INVADED

The Intentional Destruction of the
American Immigration System

J. J. CARRELL

Invaded:
The Intentional Destruction of the American Immigration System
© 2023 by John James Carrell
All Rights Reserved

No part of this book may be reproduced, stored in a retrieval system, or transmitted by any means without the written permission of the author and publisher.

Published in the United States of America
1 2 3 4 5 6 7 8 9 10

I dedicate this book to the past and current Border Patrol Agents that stand guard to protect our great nation.

CONTENTS

Prologue vii
Chapter 1   The Border Is Alive 1
Chapter 2   The Border Present Day: CHAOS 13
Chapter 3   Trump vs. All Presidents 31
Chapter 4   Mayorkas 48
Chapter 5   How Did We Get Here? 62
Chapter 6   Show Us Respect! We Demand it! 77
Chapter 7   Why? 91
Chapter 8   How? 104
Chapter 9   The Other Borders 117
Chapter 10   "How?" Part II: ICE 133
Chapter 11   NGOs: Smugglers 141
Chapter 12   Drugs, Disease, and Death 150
Chapter 13   Environmental Disaster 161
Chapter 14   Standing Army of Criminal Aliens 171
Chapter 15   Manifestation of Treason 181
Chapter 16   Sexual Abuse/Child Exploitation 190
Chapter 17   Finalizing the Smuggle: AMNESTY ... 199
Chapter 18   Leadership 208
Chapter 19   The Solutions 218
Endnotes 225
About the Author 237

PROLOGUE

I STRONGLY BELIEVE THAT while you are reading this book, you will understand from where my point of view and perspective comes. As important as it is to know who I am, it is equally important to know who I am not. I am not a disgruntled government employee, a union agitator, or someone trying to even a score. Instead, I have great pride in the United States Border Patrol and my twenty-four-year career as a Journeyman Agent, Supervisory Agent, and Deputy Patrol Agent in Charge. I also cherish the relationships I have with former colleagues, because those relationships were forged during violent, dark, yet exhilarating times.

I have a different perspective because of my unique experience being a front-line Agent in the border war—and it is a war! My experience supervising courageous and patriotic Border Patrol Agents in battle along the southern border and up the Pacific coastline gave me tremendous insight into the character of these men and women in green. Finally, during my time as a Watch Commander, and then as a senior leader with the title of Deputy Patrol Agent in Charge, I participated in the meetings and discussions about our law enforcement posture in San Diego Sector. It afforded me the opportunity to have a say in the deployment of funds, people, and equipment. I had a thirty-thousand-foot view. However, toward the end of my career, it also provided me insight that confirmed my decades-long belief that lawless men have been conspiring to destroy the American immigration system.

I spent my first decade in the Border Patrol at the Imperial Beach Border Patrol Station. I started in 1997 as a new trainee, later promoted to Supervisory Border Patrol Agent. This decade on the border was one of the most violent times in the recent history of the Border Patrol. I made my bones and earned a reputation as a hardworking and productive Agent. I am most proud of my reputation as the Agent you wanted coming to back you up when you were struggling for your life. I also had the reputation as the Supervisor you wanted at your side when things went sideways, and things always went sideways. As a young Agent and Supervisor, those years on the border were life-changing, constantly testing my ability to stand firm in the face of adversity, violence, and political corruption. I was forced by the men I arrested to do things in the dark of night that make people uncomfortable when spoken about, but I will never apologize to anyone for how I kept America and her citizens safe. The men and women that worked with and for me are heroes. We are in a war on the border with hardened criminals, smugglers of humans and narcotics, and most ardently with traitors within our own government.

My career spanned the presidential administrations of Clinton, Bush, Obama, Trump, and—when I finally retired in 2021—Biden. Aside from Trump, every other president and his administration used immigration as a weapon against America. Each one of those men manipulated immigration laws and policies to overwhelm the immigration system. These presidents played political games with border funding, ultimately leaving America open to criminal aliens, narcotics, and millions of individuals who have crushed our social services, education, hospitals, culture, and maimed and killed our citizens. None have caused more destruction through criminal conspiracy than Biden and his traitorous administration.

I will articulate in detail how our nation has come to this point in our history, where millions upon millions of illegal aliens are being encouraged and facilitated to enter our country through fraudulent channels. I will expose the manipulation of immigration policies, as well as name the traitors who have created these unlawful loopholes. I will show the manifestation of these criminal actions and the destruction of the American way of life as crime explodes and social services are stretched to the breaking point. I will write about uncomfortable topics which will result in screams of racism There will be over fifty million foreign-born residents living in America—both legal and illegal immigrants—by 2024. We must ask difficult questions. Did Americans vote for a complete shift in demographics? When did Americans vote for open borders, allowing individuals from around the globe to enter our country illegally? When did Americans vote for foreigners to have special treatment and access to America's treasure and security?

The answer is that Americans never voted for this. Politicians from both parties, in collusion with big corporations and activist groups, have usurped the American voice and power, and then told us all to sit down and shut up.

I will not sit down, nor will I shut up. Instead, in this book I will lay out how the destruction of the American immigration system is negatively altering our way of life, how it is destroying our culture, and how it is eviscerating our security as individuals and our sovereignty as a nation. The politicians and elites have made America vulnerable, and they are selling every piece of her for votes and money which create unlimited power for themselves.

The demographic shift that is occurring is not just racial or ethnic—it is a shift from citizens to non-citizens. Non-citizens are easier to control and manipulate because they are solely dependent on the same politicians who let them into our nation. This demographic shift is happening at an unprecedented speed: by the end of Biden's term in office, he will have let in twenty to thirty million illegal aliens by fraudulent immigration policies and through the hundreds of miles of open borders which allow millions to cross it undetected.

The greatest threats to America are not China, Russia, or the failing economy. America's greatest enemies are the traitors within our government who are intentionally destroying our immigration system. America's politicians and elites are flooding our nation with millions of individuals that do not share our language or culture. Simple math shows that if America continues down this path, she will be so changed from within that she will no longer be the greatest nation on earth.

CHAPTER 1
The Border Is Alive

IN ORDER TO tell this story of our own government's effort to destroy the border and the American immigration system, I must tell you that the border is not just a place where people cross from one nation to another. The border is a country all her own. The border is a living and breathing creature, with a personality that is heartless and brutal, for both the criminals crossing the border and for the law-enforcement agents protecting America. The border's appearance is harsh, dirty, and unsophisticated. The border loves violence and encourages the worst in people. The border has no compassion and shows no remorse for the pain and suffering that occurs on her land. The border tests the fears of the men and women that cross and challenges the Border Patrol Agents to internalize their frustrations and feelings of betrayal into positive actions to secure America's borders. The border will punish everyone who stands on her. I learned very early on in my career that the border was not my friend, but a place to endure.

When I see an old picture from my Border Patrol career or when a video on cable news shows a large group of illegal aliens running away from Border Patrol Agents, I swear all my senses come to life as if I am transported back to that crazy world. The world of the border is so real and so intense that every aspect of it—from her scent to the colors of the hills, to the sounds and the way my body felt—is still so raw for me.

San Diego Sector Border Patrol Agent.

The air on the border is so polluted that it feels thick, like it is carrying dirt with it. Dust covers everything in a soft, filthy film. The moment you step on the border, you feel dirty. To me it felt like the actual land moved—like a chest moves when it takes in air and then exhales it. This creature did not discriminate against Agents, illegal criminals, smugglers, or people seeking a better life; the only group of people the border seemed to oppress more than others were the weak. All the players on the border hated the weak, including the Agents.

It would not be fair to look at the border from just my perspective, ignoring the other side. Every person that has lived on, worked on, and used the border as a passageway into America has a perspective and a voice in the description of the border. I am assuming, and I could be wrong, that I would not agree much with Dr. Norma Cantu, an associate professor of English at Laredo State University. Not only does she hold a PhD, but she is also a published author of poetry, short fiction, and critical analysis. Dr. Cantu's article titled, "Living on the Border: A Wound That Will Not Heal,"[1] articulates perfectly the other side's perspective:

> The pain and joy of the borderlands—perhaps no greater or lesser than the emotions stirred by the living anywhere contradictions abound, cultures clash and meld, and life is lived on an edge—come from a wound that will not heal and yet is forever healing. These lands have always been here: the river of people has flowed for centuries. It is only the designation "border" that is relatively new, and along with the term comes the life one lives in this "in-between world" that makes us the "other," the marginalized. But, from our perspective, the "other" is outside, away from, and alien to, the border. This is our reality, and we, especially we Chicanos and Chicanas, negotiate it in our daily lives, as we contend with being treated as aliens ourselves. This in essence is the greatest wound: the constant reminder of our otherness.

I do not have to agree with the other side's perspective on any level, but it does not change the fact that their perspective and beliefs are their truth, and this plays a key role in the tension and angst felt on the border. Dr. Cantu is correct in her description of the border as a wound. There has been and continues to be immense pain inflicted by this living piece of earth.

I can remember sitting with my ATV Unit on top of Spooner's Mesa, a large flat area on a hill right next to the border and about a half a mile from the Pacific Ocean. Spooner's Mesa is a beautiful location because it is one of the highest points on the west side of the San Ysidro Port of Entry. The sunsets were amazing, but they also signaled that night was coming, which always brought excitement. On a clear day, you could see all the way to Point Loma, California and the million-dollar homes just two miles away in Coronado, California. The irony was that four hundred yards south of the northern edge of Spooner's Mesa was the steel landing mat fence that made the border wall. Two miles as the crow flies north was unimaginable wealth, and four hundred yards south was poverty and misery, all separated by a steel fence, and us. Sitting there looking out at the beauty of San Diego, I confirmed my strongly held belief that the average person has no idea what the border is like. People live in expensive bubbles in America, and the border might as well be on the planet Mars. And many times, it felt like another planet.

North edge of Spooner's Mesa overlooking San Diego skyline.

The border terrain in Imperial Beach is unique, difficult to navigate, and dangerous. I left a lot of myself on that border. Living in Southern California was and is extremely expensive; as a new Agent, I would work an extra shift every week to earn a little extra money. When I worked midnight shift, I would come in at 2:00 p.m. to start an eight-hour swing shift for overtime. On this particular double shift that started at 2:00 p.m., I was assigned my midnight shift position on East Spooner's Mesa. There were several tree lines on Spooner's that ran north and south and led into two deep canyons: one called the 24 Draw, the other directly north of East Spooner's Mesa position was the 33 Draw. The 24 Draw went straight down about seventy-five feet onto rocks. Anyone falling into that draw was going to meet his maker. The entrance of the 33 Draw had a deep undercut where illegal aliens would hide, then slowly make their way down into the deep canyon, some fifty to seventy-five feet down. The sides of the 33 Draw are grassy, with a small tree or two growing out of the side of the draw. Both the 24 and 33 Draws make Agents hesitate and take it slow.

The 33 Draw was over four hundred yards long from the top to the bottom. The trail at the bottom of the draw was extremely narrow, and several junctions would allow only one person to squeeze through at a time. Once an individual, or large group of illegal aliens, made it to the bottom, it was a hard sprint, covering three hundred yards through an open field, to the polluted Tijuana River, where the odds tilted to the illegal alien's favor. One particular night I will never forget. I was sitting on a small hill where the East Spooner's Mesa unit sat when I heard a sensor called by our dispatch. The sensor was behind me at the top of the 33 Draw. Our Inside Infrared Scope Operator could see the northern face of Spooner's Mesa, and the operator called out a group of eleven making their way into the draw. I drove my Border Patrol vehicle off the little hill I was sitting on to the top of the 33 Draw which sat a few hundred yards to my north. As I exited my vehicle and ran to the top of the draw, the Inside Scope Operator radioed to me that I was at the group's "last had," meaning the Inside Scope Operator had lost sight of the group as they entered the 33 Draw. I could hear them climbing down the sides of the canyon and jumping onto landing spots, trying to get to the base of the canyon so they could move faster. I knew that I couldn't get down the same way the group had traveled, so I went on the west side of the draw and walked the ridge line, trying to look down where the illegal aliens would be moving. It was damp that night; the fog and mist seemed to always create a wet dew on the grass and bushes. The farther north I moved along the west side, the thicker the fog got. I stepped farther east to get a better look into the canyon, but I was shocked to see that the edge of the canyon was right under my feet. The last thing I remember was telling myself that I needed to move away from the edge, but I didn't move fast enough. The ground beneath my feet crumbled under my weight, and I fell thirty-five feet straight down into the rocky bottom of the draw.

I was knocked out, and when I opened my eyes, I was sitting upright, with my back against the canyon wall. Dirt was falling around me, and my first thought was that I had fallen asleep in my vehicle and was having a bad dream. That's when the pain began to throb in my head and back, and I heard other Agents yelling my name. I was not dreaming; I had cracked open the back of my head and suffered a deep gash over my left eye, but the real pain came from a broken tail bone. I couldn't move at all and needed help badly. I sat there bleeding and angry at myself for being in this position. I could hear Agents faintly calling to me, as they were climbing up the steep draw from the north of the canyon to help me.

Six Agents made it to me, and I remember two of them to this day: Patty, a Senior Agent who was tough as nails, and Bill, a badass Supervisor. They had a hardboard stretcher which they strapped me onto and then lifted all six feet three inches and 215 pounds of me up and over their heads, to navigate the narrow and windy trail leading out of the 33 Draw. I will never forget being strapped onto that board, with my head stabilized, so all I could see were the sides of the canyon at the top and the heavy fog floating above me. These Agents carried me all the way down, taking turns maneuvering the twists and turns of the canyon trail and handing me off to each other in order to make it to the north end of the draw. Those Agents were heroes to me that night.

Top of the 33 Draw. Credit: Dave Ellrod/EllrodImages.

The border made me acutely aware that I needed to show it much more respect. When I made it back to full duty, I retained my aggressiveness, but I now had a better understanding and respect that the place I worked at was a living, breathing animal. Desperation and hopelessness are the driving characteristics of the border. The transvestites servicing their clients, then cleaning themselves in the polluted Tijuana River; the glue heads and the paint sniffers with silver or gold paint splashed across their faces, with their wild and crazed eyes; the heroin junkies sharing needles to pump their veins full of death; the "pollos" who were constantly abused by the coyotes smuggling them across and then through the border trails, being treated like cattle herded across the open fields—all were powerful examples of the desperation.

The violence trumped all other aspects of the border. Violence was the currency between the smugglers and their "pollos," but more importantly violence was the currency between the illegal aliens and the Agents. If you were going to be a successful Border Patrol Agent, you had to be willing to surpass the violence of your adversary. I had no hesitation surpassing the needed violence to win. I did what I had to do to survive, and I will never apologize for that!

My aggressive style and my fast decisions saved me from having to use my service weapon during my career. I pulled it out of my holster many times but never pulled the trigger—thank God. The money from smuggling, the drug-addicted smugglers, the constant assaults, objects thrown at you, deaths of illegal aliens, severe injuries to Agents—all created an environment of turmoil, fear, and intimidation.

Each shift would bring a new challenge. Once, I was working on ATVs around Stewart's Bridge, which is just a few feet from the border in an area called The South Levee—a narrow piece of the border that is smashed between the landing mat fence on the border and a concrete pilon fence fifty feet from the border. It creates a no-man's-land and a deadly funnel of violence. On that day a smuggler tried to run two illegal aliens under the bridge, past the Stewart's Bridge position. The bridge was about five feet high, and just north of it were three culverts about five feet high by ten feet wide and about twenty feet long. I got a call from the Stewart's Bridge Agent that bodies had gotten past his position. I was radioing that I was already north of his position when I spotted the three of them. The Stewart's Bridge Agent was able to arrest the two smuggled aliens hiding in the rocks, and I took off on my ATV after the smuggler as he tried to run back through the culverts and back to Mexico. I drove my ATV right up to the rocks leading into the culverts, a little ahead of the smuggler. I jumped off my ATV as he raced by, took a huge step, climbed the rocks leading to the culverts, and lunged at him as we both landed hard inside the concrete culvert. We were both on our sides as the smuggler started punching me and trying to get away. We traded blows several times and I was able to get on top of him, but something flew past my face and exploded against the concrete wall. I looked up—another smuggler had climbed over the border fence and into the concrete open area past the bridge but was still about twenty feet from the culvert where we were fighting. He threw another large piece of broken concrete at me and missed again, but only by inches.

As I straddled the smuggler beneath me, I pulled my weapon and aimed at the most recent threat. As I got him in my gun sights, the smuggler underneath me began to grab at my elbows, then my wrists, and finally at my hands, trying to wrestle away my weapon. Again, another piece of broken concrete smashed against the wall as the smuggler beneath me began punching me and grabbing my hands that were holding my gun. I knew I had to remove one of the threats and the man underneath me trying to take my gun was the closest threat of violence to me. As we struggled, I was able to spin his body on his side. Another piece of concrete smashed against the wall, making a loud explosive noise inside the concrete tunnel. I pulled my gun back to my chest, then pushed it back hard into the base of the smuggler's head and began to pull the trigger. I remember as if it was yesterday, thinking to myself as I pulled the trigger, "Man, this is going to be loud." Suddenly, the smuggler—feeling the barrel of the gun at the base of his head—threw his hands and arms straight out, giving up. The other smuggler saw my weapon, turned, and began running back to the border fence and Mexico. That was what the border would throw at you: a fight with two smugglers at the beginning of a shift. In broad daylight. The good and the bad of being a Border Patrol Agent blend. Fighting for your life is frightening and unnerving, but at the same time it is exhilarating. The true normal in the Border Patrol is the extreme threat of violence and how you react to it.

Stewart's Bridge. Credit: Dave Ellrod/EllrodImages.

I worked in the eastern sectors of California and in Douglas and Nogales, Arizona, during some of the craziest times in those areas. I remember working in Calexico, CA: running through the streets of this dirty little border town chasing illegal aliens at 1:00 a.m. Even at one in the morning, the temperature exceeded one hundred degrees in this desert town, and I was soaking wet from sweat. Nogales is a dump of a border town, and when I was there, it didn't matter if it was in the middle of the night or eleven in the morning, hundreds if not thousands of illegal aliens were running wild through the streets and climbing out of sewers and manhole covers. In Douglas, Arizona the situation was so bad that, when we would get off shift and were driving the forty-five miles back to our hotel, we would have to put on blinders and drive past hundreds of illegal aliens running up the highway north of the port of entry. If we stopped every time we saw large groups of illegal aliens, we would have worked every hour of every day of our thirty-day detail. It was in Douglas that I arrested the largest group in my career by myself: fifty-three.

The border changes shape, size, and depth along its two thousand miles from California to Arizona to New Mexico to Texas, but the violence, hopelessness, and harsh unforgiving human suffering from rape, murder, and shocking abuse is everywhere. Stories that will never be told are buried with the bodies, because, sadly, human life is worthless on the border. The pain is real. The suffering is real. The neglect from governments on both sides of the border is real.

I have become desensitized to it all. I wish I could have safeguarded better my natural human feelings of sympathy and empathy; they were stolen from me. But I also knew they have no place in my career. I would have lost my mind if I had to emotionally process every atrocity I witnessed on the border and the betrayal from our leaders, while witnessing their accumulation of corrupt wealth and power.

When you watch talking heads on cable news, read academic articles, or listen to people discuss border issues who have never set foot on that filthy and agitated piece of land, remember that the border is a place void of humanity. It is a place where suffering is expected and hope does not exist, where corruption and evil reigns. It is, as Dr. Cantu described it, a "wound." Sadly, for the Patrol it is also a place where the souls of Agents that took their own lives rest. Sometimes I wonder what it says about me that I thrived in that world.

CHAPTER 2
The Border Present Day: CHAOS

As I sit and type this chapter, I can state without reservation that there are thousands of illegal aliens sitting on our side of the border with their luggage, waiting for Border Patrol vans and buses to pick them up. Thousands of illegal aliens have already been arrested in the past twenty-four hours, and tens of thousands wait to cross the border in the coming days. Further south, hundreds of thousands of future illegal entrants begin the trek through the countries of South and Central America and into Mexico, to their illegal crossings into the United States of America. Meanwhile, millions of individuals from every country on the globe are starting their journey to Central America, and then to Mexico.

As you read this, there are hundreds of miles of the almost two thousand miles of the southern border where there is not one United States Border Patrol Agent. The Secretary of Homeland Security, Alejandro Mayorkas, blatantly lies when he states that the border is secure. Mayorkas is America's "Bagdad Bob," a propagandist and a liar (although it is insulting to compare Bagdad Bob to Mayorkas, because Bagdad Bob loved his country). The opposite is true—the border is completely and purposefully wide open.

When something is as obviously wrong as an open border, you must ask why is it not being fixed? Imagine having a huge hole in the roof of your house. It begins to rain, and water pours into your home. Everyone in your home is wet and cold, but you do nothing. The rain increases and you still do nothing. In fact, as your wife and children shiver from being soaking wet, you do the unthinkable: you climb onto your roof and make the hole bigger.

That is what your government is doing to the border, America, and her citizens.

I just received an intelligence report from one of my sources in the DHS. In this report it showed the daily twenty-four-hour arrest numbers, which totaled slightly over nine thousand, with all Border Patrol holding facilities at maximum capacity. These nine thousand arrests are actually "give ups": individuals and families that simply walked, climbed, or swam across the international border and squatted with their luggage, waiting to be picked up by the Border Patrol. Nearly all of these nine thousand "give ups" are released directly into the United States on their own recognizance, or through a Non-Governmental Organization (NGO). Either way, they are released with no follow up. The media and the Biden White House simply ignore this dire situation, pretending that this is normal.

To show how abnormal this situation is, let's compare it to Great Britain, which is averaging five thousand illegally entering boat migrants monthly. Great Britain has called for a state of emergency, stating that their country can't handle this invasion. The US Border Patrol arrests five thousand people before noon *every day* (not counting the thousands that abscond undetected daily), and not a word of concern from Biden or the corrupt media.

Let's look at one of the five thousand arrests the Border Patrol makes during the first half of the day. Let's take a Haitian family of four: a dad, mom and two young children. This family is arrested and transported to the nearest Border Patrol station and enrolled into the Department of Homeland Security Immigration Database. The father of the family will make a fraudulent claim for asylum for his entire family. The Border Patrol Agent will ask where their final destination will be, and the Haitian father will give the Agent an address in Nashville. Now, there is no way for the Agent to verify that this address exists. The Agent wants to contest the Haitian's stated destination, but he looks over to the holding cells, and the windows are sweating from the mass of humanity squeezed inside. The Agent knows he must rush to complete this family's casework, as there are hundreds of other illegal aliens being transported to his station and into the station's overcrowded holding facility where they will be processed. The Agent is forced to take the word of the Haitian man, and then provides this man and his family a Notice to Appear (NTA). This NTA is a government form that directs the family to appear before an Immigration Judge, at a certain location, on a certain date and time. Unfortunately, the backlog to see an Immigration Judge is now over six years and growing daily. So, the Agent basically gives the Haitian a blank NTA with no dates or times and instructs him that the United States government will send future correspondence to his residence in Nashville. The Haitian family is either turned over to an NGO and released later, or the Haitian family is dropped off at the nearest bus station. Either way, this family will never be seen again.

Stop for a second and let the absurdity of what you just read sink in. Now take that insane situation and multiply it by nine thousand a day. Now, take that nine thousand and multiply it by 365. You have replicated that absurd situation over three million times in one year. Heading into the third year of Biden's administration, the number of illegal aliens that will be arrested will surpass all annual records. In Biden's first two years, the Border Patrol arrested approximately 5 million individuals, with the vast majority being released exactly as I described above. Border arrests are estimated to be over 3.25 million in 2023, and all these 3.25 million will be released. The numbers increase just like the water pouring into the home with a hole in the roof. And just like the homeowner making the hole in the roof bigger, Biden makes the holes in both the border and in immigration policy and procedure bigger. The only endgame is destruction.

The border is in complete chaos, and the chaos has been created by design. None of this occurred by accident, or because of bad policy. Once I lay out how the Biden administration has encouraged, enticed, and facilitated millions of illegal aliens to cross into America, the only rational reason for this behavior is that it was orchestrated and intentionally created. (I do not pretend to believe Biden knows what planet he is on, much less what is happening on the border, so when I say Biden, I mean the conspirators within his administration and the people helping Joe tie his shoes.)

As unbelievable as the scenario I just described is, consider another daily scenario in which Agents are forced to participate. Because every Border Patrol and Immigration and Customs Enforcement (ICE) facility is overcrowded, Agents are forced to process these same illegal aliens *without* an NTA and release them into the United States. The illegal aliens are now being instructed to go to their factitious new address and wait for ICE to mail an NTA. This process shortens the time in custody, allowing Agents to quickly release these individuals. Instead of creating a NTA immigration file on our Haitians, that Agent enters simple biographical information into the DHS database and releases them right onto the street. The Border Patrol Agent then forwards the Haitian family's information to ICE Officers, who in turn mail the NTAs to the made-up addresses in Anytown, USA. ICE Officers tell me that all these mailings are returned to the ICE facility with US Postal Service stamped "Return to Sender." They also tell me that they are so overwhelmed by the endless paperwork and by transporting individuals that there are no officers monitoring these fraudulent addresses. "There is no follow-up…. They are just gone in the wind!" I expect within a very short time that Border Patrol Agents will make arrests in the field, take illegal aliens' biographical information with no verification that the information is true, and then release them on the spot.

This intentional chaos is having a severe impact on local communities across America. ICE has now published its arrest numbers for FY 2022, and they are abysmal:[2] ICE arrested fewer than thirty-three thousand illegal aliens. The arrest numbers for 2021 were no better: less than thirty-two thousand. How does that compare to Trump in FY 2018? Well, Trump's ICE arrested and deported over ninety-five thousand illegal aliens in FY18.

ICE interior enforcement is now non-existent, just as Border Patrol law enforcement activities on the border have diminished to a nominal presence. Every decision regarding law enforcement posture is to curtail and eliminate proactive law enforcement. Several ICE Supervisors tell me with complete frustration and disbelief, "I have never seen anything like this in my career. And we are doing nothing to stop it!"

The Biden administration has removed all interior enforcement. As I write this, there are over 4.8 million illegal aliens living in our country that have either a deportation order or a pending deportation order.[3] These are people who have been given every opportunity to go before an Immigration Judge while they exhaust all asylum and other fraudulent claims, while utilizing taxpayer funds to employ immigration lawyers, and are still found to be in the country illegally. They have been ordered deported and refused to leave. Many of these 4.8 million illegal aliens were ordered deported "in absentia," meaning that many of them were given a court date but did not show up. As millions cross our border and are given NTAs, asylum court dates, and are paroled, what percentage will not show up for their court dates?

And why not, because who is going to locate them? My sources throughout the DHS confidently state that almost all these people will abscond into America, never stepping foot inside an immigration court of law. The ones who do appear and want to see an Immigration Judge will wait a decade or more.

There are millions of individuals in our country who have been ordered by our government, which is us, to leave. These same individuals snub their noses and laugh at us. They do not respect our country, our laws, or our order. What outcome would a rational person conclude would happen if 4.8 million people ignored a sovereign nation's demand? A rational person would rightly conclude chaos and lawlessness would begin to reign in that nation.

It is extremely hard to follow and understand the quickly changing Border Patrol policies and manipulation of immigration laws. This is done on purpose. It is illegal, but the Biden administration does not care because who is going to hold it accountable—the Republicans?

I just received a call from a former colleague in San Diego Sector. He told me that they are now ordered to begin to minimize the use of NTAs and must use the Immigration Parole system. The rarely used Immigration Parole is completely different from state and local parole used for our prison population. It was created and is used to bring in foreign nationals to testify as a material witness to a crime, or under special humanitarian requests like a foreign national attending a family member's funeral. Border Patrol Agents are paroling illegal aliens into our country using a system that was not created or designed to be utilized in this fashion. Using Parole to quickly process and release illegal aliens is a violation of the law and is grossly immoral.

Let me explain by using the previous example of the Haitian family. Instead of this Haitian family being given a NTA, it is given a sheet of paper stating that this family has been paroled into the United States. On this piece of paper are the instructions that they must present themselves to an ICE facility at their final destination, Nashville, within sixty days. Remember that ICE facilities are overrun beyond imagination and ICE Officers are stretched beyond the breaking point, so there is no one to help these Haitians if they even try to present themselves to the ICE Officers. So, what happens to this family and the millions of illegal aliens coming into America this year, who do not or cannot present themselves to ICE? They all become "out of status" and they are considered illegal aliens.

Our government enticed and welcomed these people into our country then used them as pawns by subjecting them to receive no legal status.

I will explain more about Immigration Parole in a later chapter, but look at what our government has created. Millions upon millions of individuals illegally in our country who cannot work legally because they have no work authorization documents. Our government intentionally created a slave class of workers. These people will labor for diminished wages, be treated unfairly, and have no recourse to their grievances.

Every ICE and Border Patrol holding facility is at capacity. The "cages" the Democrats raged about under Trump are now okay under Biden. However, these "cages" are now holding double, triple, or even quadruple the capacity. "Holding cages" in Texas, for example, have capacity for four hundred individuals but now are forced to hold fourteen hundred. Minors are being held in "pods" that are thirty-two hundred square feet, and these "pods" are holding five hundred children![4] An average house in America is under thirty-two hundred square feet, but you sure as hell won't see a family of five hundred living there. Sexual abuses of children and young teenagers occur daily in these "pods." There are few if any monitors, and often the monitors are volunteers from other federal agencies with no professional training as corrections or law enforcement officers. To combat any criticism or chance the media would ever report on these conditions, the government's answer is to simply release as many people as possible.

I have a former colleague that is a Supervisor in Eagle Pass Sector in southern Texas that would contact me and tell me how he just "street released" eight hundred people into the city of San Antonio. "Street Release" means Border Patrol Agents load up as many buses as they have and drive to the nearest city and dump them on the street. This Supervisor told me that their Area of Operation (AOR) is unpatrolled and busting at the seams with thousands upon thousands of illegal aliens pouring across the border undetected. This Supervisor also made sure that I understood that the moment they street-released hundreds of illegal aliens into a community, their holding facility would be back to maximum capacity before the buses even returned to the Border Patrol station.

The numbers of Unaccompanied Alien Children (UAC) has exploded under Biden, and so has the number of sexual assaults and rapes of young children, both on the other side of the border and in our DHS custody. The hypocrisy is so blatant, when you compare what then-Vice-President Biden said in 2014, when he visited Guatemala City, stating,

> The United States, to state the obvious, is greatly concerned by the startling number of unaccompanied minors that—children and teenagers who are making a very perilous journey through Central America to reach the United States. These are some of the most vulnerable migrants that ever attempt—and many from around the world attempt—to come to the United States. They're among the most vulnerable. And the majority of these individuals rely—we estimate between 75 and 80 percent—rely on very dangerous, not-nice, human-smuggling networks that transport them through Central America and Mexico to the United States.

> These smugglers—and everyone should know it, and not turn a blind eye to it—these smugglers routinely engage in physical and sexual abuse, and extortion of these innocent, young women and men by and large.
>
> And they profit from the misery of these children and teenagers; these desperate, desperate young people.[5]

Now, as the "cages" are filled past capacity and Biden and his traitorous team have "lost" over eighty-five thousand UACs, Biden says nothing.

Across Texas, New Mexico, Arizona, and California, there are miles of unprotected and unmanned border. One Supervisor recently told me that they are arresting only the people who give themselves up. The ones that are criminals are running through the open border areas. One Supervisor on detail to Yuma Sector told me in complete exasperation, "J. J., there is no one patrolling the border. No one!" I questioned what areas of Yuma Sector's 126 miles of responsibility was left unmanned and he shouted, "All of them!" After everything I have experienced throughout my career, even I was stunned that not only were all 126 miles left open, but also that this is the case across the Border Patrol Sectors along the southern border. Things have gotten so bad in Yuma that entering 2022 and into 2023, the mayor has declared a state of emergency.[6] Directly from Yuma's own website, Mayor Douglas Nicholls explained, "I have maintained the City's emergency proclamation in force for the last year because there have been no significant changes in policy or procedures from the Department of Homeland

Security to reduce the flow of people crossing the border."[7] San Diego Sector was the closest to being fortified with walls, technology, and infrastructure with limited crossings, but now tens of thousands of getaways monthly are claimed. A Supervisor called me recently and told me that he had just got off shift and there were eight hundred getaways just on his midnight shift. That's what Agents can account for; as he told me, that number could easily be sixteen hundred or more, and that is in just one station on one shift!

The Biden administration and the leaders of DHS are moving these illegal aliens across the southern border to be processed and to hide the numbers. Illegal aliens are being bussed and flown from one American border state to another. A Patrol Agent in Charge of one of the seven San Diego Border Patrol Stations texted me in disbelief when a bus arrived from Arizona carrying fifty illegal aliens from nineteen different countries speaking eleven different languages. This station is in constant turmoil because of the lack of staffing, and the constant intake and releasing of hundreds of illegal aliens. Before the Biden administration, Imperial Beach Station's lowest staffing levels were once fifty Agents a shift to work in the field. Several Agents from the Imperial Beach Station in San Diego Sector texted me that now their law enforcement staffing is usually at five Agents per shift to work in the field, and once or twice the staffing in the field was at two. That means that the Imperial Beach Station—directly north of the violent Mexican city of Tijuana—is completely unprotected. Most of the Agent's time is spent transporting and processing. They have no idea or concept of what their duties and responsibilities are now under this DHS leadership.

Overlooking the east side of Imperial Beach Station AOR.

I speak daily with my former colleagues and sources. They are lost, frustrated, angry, and embarrassed, but there is a new emotion I have never seen in Border Patrol Agents and ICE Officers: fear. They all say, with gripping fear, "I have never seen anything like this in my career." There is always a long pause, then they finish, "But we are doing nothing to stop it…nothing!"

The insanity goes even beyond "just releasing them." Over 350,000 illegal aliens have been released into our country under a program called Alternatives to Detention (ATD)[8], devised to be a pressure release value to continue to facilitate the flow of illegal aliens into our nation. Every ICE and Border Patrol holding facility is over maximum capacity. Court dates are booked into 2030, but, in fact, hundreds of thousands of illegal aliens' court dates are not even on the docket. Because of the purposeful court backlog, ATD is the quickest and most efficient way to move these illegal aliens out of these overcrowded facilities and to create more space for the millions of illegal aliens that are crossing and or preparing to cross. The agency within ICE that is tasked with ATD is Enforcement and Removal Operations (ERO), which is tasked with monitoring over 350,000 illegal aliens in this program. ERO places ankle bracelets on these illegal aliens, or—get this!—provide each one with a new iPhone that will be their tracking device. My source in ICE just laughed when I asked about this monitoring. "There is no one monitoring ATD. We are drowning in the corruption." I confirmed with other Border Patrol Agents on reports of ATD tracking bracelets left in trash cans, or bathrooms of bus stations, along the southern border.

The president and his administration do not have the authority to manipulate immigration law, which states that all illegal aliens must wait in their home countries, or countries outside of the United States, for their immigration hearings to determine status.

Instead of following the law, Biden makes new law out of whole cloth. The Republicans stand by and pretend to care, while participating in this crime. They are not fighting for America; I confidently and correctly argue that the Republicans are players in this corruption—they gain wealth and power just like the Democrats.

The average American looks at ATD and thinks, "Well, at least the government knows who they released and where these individuals are." Well, not so fast. In September of 2022, Syracuse University's research group called Transactional Research Access Clearinghouse (TRAC) filed a Freedom of Information Act (FOIA) request with the DHS, requesting to secure the information on the more than 350,000 individuals enrolled in the ATD program from fiscal year 2019 to August

2022.[9] DHS responded to TRAC's FOIA request with an astonishing statement:

> You have requested records pertaining to "the latest alien-by-alien, anonymous data covering all individuals who were taken into custody by ICE and entered (or transferred to) ICE ATD custody from the beginning of FY 2019 through August 2022 (or date of search, whichever later). ICE has conducted a search of the ICE Enforcement and Removal Operations (ERO) for records responsive to your request and *no records responsive to your request were found* (emphasis added).

Read that again! DHS, under Mayorkas, has no records on over 350,000 illegal aliens that were released under the ATD program. This number of 350,000 is a fraction of the nearly five million individuals arrested and eventually released under Biden's first two years in office, but 350,000 individuals, with no records of who or where they are, is a staggering number.

My former colleagues I speak with are law enforcement professionals who have been in the thick of it for decades, and they are often speechless trying to describe the situation on the border. When they describe their daily tasks, law enforcement is never discussed. They have become the facilitators of the final piece of the smuggling operation. No longer does a car or van pull up alongside the highway or along some dense brush to pick up their loads to smuggle north to deliver their "pollos" to the stash houses. Instead, it is these professional law enforcement officers that are taking the illegal aliens from the station or from the field and driving them to the illegal alien's final destination. Agents once deported these very same illegal aliens. Now these same Agents are not deporting them, but are actually giving them new iPhones, bus or plane tickets, and some even get preloaded cash cards. Every single one of the millions being released gets one or all of these goodies.

The quiet part of this open border strategy is the volume of hard narcotics pouring into our country. At the end of President Trump's term there was an epidemic of 50,000 drug overdose deaths annually, especially fentanyl, which is used to cut and mix with hard narcotics like cocaine and heroin—a staggering number equal to the total death toll from the Vietnam War: EVERY YEAR! Fast forward to today, and two years into the Biden Presidency that number has surpassed 100,000 and is careening toward 150,000 overdose deaths annually.

I can draw a straight line from the open borders directly to the overdose deaths. The Mexican drug cartels are making billions, transporting not only narcotics but people, guns, and whatever else American citizens demand, through miles and miles of open borders without fear. They create chaos by having the minimum law enforcement staffing detain, transport and process large groups of illegal aliens they, the cartels, move like chess pieces along the border. No one crosses the border without the cartel's approval or payment. The hordes of humanity that you see on television did not just decide to cross and squat in that exact spot; the cartels directed them. As Border Patrol Agents take custody of these squatters, the cartels cross their cargo beyond the Agent's sight.

Federal, state, and local law enforcement officers are making huge busts of millions of fentanyl pills both along the major border cities and in the interior states. Fentanyl deaths are rising beyond crisis levels across our major metropolitan cities and small rural towns in America.

The rule of thumb throughout my career has been for every illegal alien you arrest, at least one or two get away. As I write this, DHS has reported five million arrests in Biden's first two years of his presidency. I believe without hesitation that at least another five million illegal aliens (my extremely conservative estimate) have made it into America undetected, perhaps closer to eight to ten million.

Among the millions of illegal aliens arrested in the first two years of Biden's reign, almost one hundred have been terrorists. I take no pleasure in stating that those were the dumb terrorists, because if you think that every terrorist that crossed our open border was arrested, you are either a fool or you don't want to acknowledge the danger America is in. Even among the millions arrested and then released by Border Patrol Agents, there had to have been hundreds of terrorists released as well.

When you read a DHS report on criminals and terrorists arrested crossing the border, you must understand that the DHS is making a claim without properly explaining exactly what the data states. When an individual is entered into our national database and is checked for criminal history, that database only checks for crimes committed *in* the United States or terrorists that are on *our* watch list. We have no idea what crimes have been committed or terrorist associations these people have in their home countries. Some of these countries have no formal criminal database and they certainly do not have terrorist members walking into their nation's corrupt law enforcement stations wanting to be put on America's terrorist watch list. Do you see the danger and the absurdity of what is being portrayed to the American public—that every one of these illegal aliens has been vetted and is just a hard-working individual looking for a new life? Murderers, rapists, drug dealers, gang members, and terrorists are being arrested and released, or are getaways, in the thousands.

For the first five years of my career, the media and the government stated that there were five million illegal aliens living in the United States. However, I always strongly believed that the number was at least double that. From the sixth to the twenty-first year of my career, the number increased to eleven million. There is not one topic in politics today that every media member and every politician from both sides of the aisle agree with, but every talking head and every government employee recites the number "eleven million" as if they are quoting one of the Ten Commandments. Eleven million is sacred, never changing. Why? Because America would choke on the true number.

In 2018, Yale and MIT did a study to find the number of illegal aliens living in the country.[10] This study used data of deportations, visa overstays, and demographics to determine the number and ran it through a mathematical simulation a million times, the result being a number as low as sixteen million and as high as twenty-nine million illegal aliens living in our country. The mathematical model found the mean to be twenty-two million. I believe the true number of illegal aliens living in America to be closer to thirty million. Just these last two years under Biden makes the twenty-two million number seem ridiculously low. The Center for Immigration Studies recently claimed that the number of foreign-born (both legal and illegal immigrants) in our country is over forty-seven million.[11] If these numbers under Biden continue—and I have seen no reason why it will not—there will be over fifty million illegal aliens living in the United States of America by 2024. Ask yourself to name one country or empire in the course of human history that has survived this ratio of its residents being illegal aliens or foreign-born legal residents or citizens. The obvious answer is there is not one. If you are a rational person, the very next question asked would be, "Why is this being allowed to happen to our country?"

CHAPTER 3
Trump vs. All Presidents

For the first twenty years of my Border Patrol career, we were always losing. Whatever "plan" was in vogue to secure the border was a political ploy for more votes and wealth. Even as a new Border Patrol Agent in my twenties, nothing ever made sense. No presidential administration's plan added up. Two plus two never equaled four. What was so frustrating was the "plan" never went past step one—the true "plan" was that there was never any depth or desire to truly secure the border.

I remember driving to the Imperial Beach Border Patrol Station for the first time after graduating from the United States Border Patrol Academy. It was October 1997, and I was making a "dry run" to the station to make sure I knew the best route to take for my first day on duty. I did not want to be late. Years of playing football in high school and college had drilled into me that need to be on time and prepared. I exited off I-5 and turned down a dirty street named Hollister. As I drove, I could see the hills leading up to the border. I could see the steel landing mats from the Vietnam War used to construct our first "wall." Past the border fence, I could see a gigantic Mexican flag flapping in the wind from the center of Tijuana. The flag had to be over one hundred feet long. My heart raced as a new and exciting world was waiting for me.

My first years in the Border Patrol were a blur, as life as a Trainee/New Border Patrol Agent was one of constant learning. Those first years are where an Agent builds the foundation of his reputation. To this day, every Agent is either a Slug or a Worker. There is no in-between. God built me to work hard and to be a leader. I was a Worker, and I immediately began to make a name for myself. I loved being outside in the elements, the freedom of working alone as well as in teams, and the daily challenge to my character and toughness.

The San Diego and Southern California I lived in was once truly beautiful beyond description. Million-dollar homes, clear blue skies, and beautiful people everywhere. Driving to work further south down I-5, the beauty of Southern California would abruptly disappear as I entered the border towns of National City and Imperial Beach. Porsches, Mercedes, Bentleys, and high-dollar SUVs disappeared from the interstate, replaced by broken down Toyotas, white rusted panel vans, and strange cars made of parts from multiple car brands. I had to take several different routes to work, based on traffic, but I always ended up on Hollister Street, where the sky's color would change from the bluest blue to a strange and ominous orange, caused by the pollution in Tijuana. The smell of sewage, farmland, and mesquite brush dominated the air. The border towns on both sides of the international border are violent, dirty and crime infested. This strange world of dysfunction, chaos, and violence was my world, and as a new, young Agent, I loved it.

I remember my first month living in San Diego; I did not see a cloud in that big blue sky all month. I had just graduated from the Border Patrol Academy in Charleston, South Carolina and driven across the country to a land of beauty that I had never seen before. I remember as I crossed through each state and got closer to California, I became more and more excited.

Thirteen of us, out of fifty trainees from Academy Class 339, went to Imperial Beach Station in October of 1997. We gave ourselves the nickname "The Baker's Dozen." After the first day or two of administrative work, our Field Training Officer (FTO) took us around the Imperial Beach's AOR, which covered numerous hills, valleys, riverbeds, and endless smuggler trails, included the cities of Imperial Beach and National City, and parts of San Diego.

I remember my first arrest as if it were yesterday, and, man, I was hooked. I remember all thirteen of us with all of our gear jammed into a fifteen-passenger van driving through the old streets of Imperial Beach near the pier. We had just started our AOR training on day shift, and it was a typical beautiful sunny day of about seventy degrees. My six-foot-three frame with all my gear was somehow squeezed into the center of the first-row bench seating as my FTO began to slow down and point to two men walking slowly up the street. We were all so green that these men didn't look any different than any other two men walking down the street. That was the difference between a Senior Agent and The Baker's Dozen.

Our FTO knew that there were border trails along the Bird Sanctuary just north of the Mexico border, leading to the streets of Imperial Beach. He saw two men with muddy shoes, scuff marks on their pants, and recognized the way they walked. All it took was for our FTO to hit the brakes and yell, "Get them!" and I was off. I pushed myself over the hump between the driver's and passenger's seats, flew out of the van all in one movement onto the pavement, and I ran. Three other "nugs," as we were called, were running with me, and those poor men never stood a chance against four new Border Patrol Agents fresh out of the Academy. A simple one-hundred-yard dash, a fence jump or two, and a tackle were a warmup to us.

This was my first of hundreds of foot chases where jumping fences and tackling people became normal. But this was my first time, and first times are always special. I vividly remember jumping over a fence and landing in a backyard and seeing one of the men trying in vain to jump another fence. I rushed after him and slammed him to the ground.

Being less than a week out of the Academy, The Baker's Dozen did not know any better than what we were taught in the classroom. Role-playing arresting and searching someone in a classroom and doing the real thing in the field are night and day. These poor dudes got the full arrest and search treatment. We searched through all their clothes, their shoes, their hair, and under their ball caps. Years later, we still laugh at how ridiculous we were in those early days of our career. Our FTO would move onto another group of trainees, and we were individually left alone to win or lose on the border. The most vivid memory of that day was how much I was sweating after making my first arrest and how proud I was!

Credit: Dave Ellrod/EllordImages.

I entered on duty in the late '90s, under President Clinton. Operation Gatekeeper was in full effect. It was an infusion of federal funds into San Diego Sector that increased manpower, infrastructure, and technology, as a trial sector to see if this new "plan" would work. Although Operation Gatekeeper was profoundly successful, the implementation of all its phases was never instituted. The "plan" was to stop the flow of thousands of illegal aliens from pouring into our country on a daily basis. Then, once the border flow was stopped, manpower would shift north into the border towns, into San Diego and beyond. Once we made our presence established in these border communities, Agents would locate, arrest, and deport the hundreds of thousands of illegal aliens living in that section of the country. Unfortunately, politicians and weak leaders within the Immigration and Naturalization Service (INS) never allowed it.

Imperial Beach Border Patrol Station has operational responsibility of six linear miles from the southwestern most point of the United States to the San Ysidro Port of Entry. Prior to Operation Gatekeeper and my arrival at the Imperial Beach Station, the border was wide open and chaotic. Imperial Beach would arrest over three thousand illegal aliens every twenty-four hours. During this same twenty-four-hour period, the Agents would physically witness up to four times that number absconded. In only six of the almost two thousand miles of the southern border, the number of getaways was estimated to be in the thousands, daily.

Southwestern point of the United States.
Credit: Dave Ellrod/EllrodImages.

Older Agents that I looked up to and tried to imitate would tell me stories of those days. Violence ruled: murders, rapes, and assaults were a daily occurrence on both sides of the border from Mexican smugglers and criminals preying on illegal aliens from every country. Agents faced being shot at, assaulted, and injured from working on the dangerous border terrain. Agents would describe having one hundred illegal aliens in custody in an open field just north of the border, as another hundred illegal aliens ran past them and the foot-guide smuggler would yell out, "*Chinga tu madre!*"

Operation Gatekeeper's ultimate goal was to tame the wild west. A border fence was created from old, rusted Vietnam landing mats. This fence would stretch across the six miles of the Imperial Beach Station's AOR. The fence stood about fifteen feet high, the landing mat panels pieced together horizontally with little foresight and planning, which meant the deep horizonal grooves of the landing mats went from one end of the panel to the other, creating a ladder. The illegal aliens would use this ladder to climb up and over the fence. But it was still better than no fence.

Hundreds of Agents were directed to the Imperial Beach Station. Technology was infused into the landscape in the form of stationary infrared cameras, mobile infrared cameras mounted on trucks, and ground sensors that detected the movement of illegal aliens and drug smugglers through the border area.

The Border Patrol and the smugglers lined up their forces, and the war to control the border began along these six miles. The smugglers of humans and narcotics ran a multimillion-dollar business within these six miles, and they were not going to close shop.

The "Old Patrol Agents" went to war every single day and fought strength with strength, violence with violence, and began to win. The tide began to shift, and by the late '90s, we had control over these six miles where the Mexican smugglers had once ruled with an iron fist and mocked the Border Patrol. However, as we finished our ten-hour shift, covered in dirt and at times blood, we would drive from this other dimension back into the world where all of us could see thousands of illegal aliens living among us, creating havoc in our communities. Murders, rapes, and assaults in border towns, San Diego, and the suburbs occurred daily. Social services were stretched, schools were failing and overcrowded, and hospital emergency rooms were filled with illegal aliens receiving free medical services. Agents fought with everything they had during Gatekeeper, because they were promised that once they controlled the border, they would be turned loose in the interior. Then, they would arrest and deport every last illegal alien.

That was a lie.

I entered on duty during the last part of Operation Gatekeeper, one of the new Agents that helped the "Old Patrol" seal off the border. I remember those days as fast, confusing, and exhilarating.

I just read a letter I sent to my dad during my second year in the Patrol, where I wrote that I could not believe that I was getting paid to do this job and how proud I was to be a Border Patrol Agent. Like many Agents, we were so in the depths of a war that politics and the real intent of the betrayal from our own government did not enter our thoughts. We were having fun and trying to stay alive. As I moved into my third then fourth years of my career, and Gatekeeper had worked, I began to question why the Border Patrol was not moving into the second and third phases of Gatekeeper. We had done the dirty and dangerous job of sealing the border and we, naively, believed we were going to clean out our communities of the hundreds of thousands of illegal aliens. Illegal alien gangs and criminals roamed San Diego and California without fear of being arrested and then deported by Border Patrol. We were all chomping at the bit to move north and impose our will. These same illegal aliens that spat on and cursed us were now going to get their justice and in turn we would make the communities we lived in safer and more prosperous.

Me as a young Supervisor!

This was a time in my career when I was able to stop, breathe, and look around at all facets of the Border Patrol, INS, and the newly formed DHS. Many times, I have wished I wasn't built to ask questions and was allowed to live in a state of ignorance, but that is not how God built me. I began to openly question why during my off-duty time I had to wade through hordes of illegal aliens in the front of Home Depot or watch hundreds of illegal aliens using our public transportation and not be allowed by our Border Patrol leadership to go back there on duty and arrest them. I was able to piece it all together and I quickly realized that the leaders of my agency were being directed to stop any and all interior enforcement. During this time, my colleagues and I would be stacked on top of each other along the border as maybe one or two individuals would try and cross the border, but thousands and thousands of illegal aliens freely moved about our cities with no fear of ever running into one of us.

I look back on this moment in my career with sadness because this is when I knew the greatest enemy I faced was not the felon that I would have to fight into submission in the dark canyons of the border, but the politicians that used and manipulated both law enforcement officers and illegal aliens as pawns, to enrich themselves with power.

I followed my father into federal law enforcement. My dad was a highly respected and successful Secret Service Agent that guarded presidents LBJ, Nixon, Ford, Carter, Reagan, Bush, and Clinton. Being a strong Catholic, the greatest assignment my dad had as a Special Agent in Charge was when Pope John Paul II visited the United States in New Orleans, and he had responsibility for the Pope's protection detail. My father has since passed, and I cherish my framed picture of my father guarding the then Pope John Paul II and now saint. To say I am proud of my dad would be a gross understatement. My dad was the truest example of what a real man was. I miss him.

I have always been a Republican. As Clinton's presidency ended, I was hopeful that a Republican president would bring an end to the dire border situation. I was still naive. I learned from continuous disappointment that there is no real difference between a Democrat and a Republican; they just maneuver on different levels of lying and deceiving American citizens. I found Bush's non-action and fence straddling on immigration even more frustrating and disappointing than Clinton's. I had no expectation of a strong enforcement plan and follow through from a Democrat, but back then I did from a Republican.

President Bush was never going to tackle the immigration situation head on, but then 9/11 hit America. The Border Patrol community was angry because we knew that the failed immigration policies and criminal malfeasance from our government was where the blame lay. Several of the 9/11 terrorists were visa overstays and had once lived in San Diego. I wondered many times if the governmental cowards had not held us back from implementing the other phases of enforcement in Operation Gatekeeper, would one of the twenty-five hundred San Diego Sector Border Patrol Agents have come across one or two of these terrorists during their interior patrol duties? Could arresting just one of these bastards have caused them to halt their horrible attack on America? We will never know, but I do know weak, cowardly, and corrupt leadership always manifests itself in sorrow, pain, and extreme disappointment.

We believed the country and her citizens had been so savagely beaten that the politicians would be forced to react to the nation's demand for security and safety, that these demands would force the politicians to unshackle immigration law enforcement officers and allow us to enforce the laws we swore an oath to defend. We waited and waited.

On September 12, 2001, the United States Border Patrol stood ready for our orders to eliminate all illegal aliens from our country. We were certain President Bush and Congress were going to take all the constraints off and finally allow us to do our job. It never happened. Instead, unbelievably, we kept doing the exact same thing. We tried to secure the border without any real plan, funding, or expectations.

We witnessed the creation of the Department of Homeland Security, and any hopes of strong leadership in this newly created department faded quickly as we did nothing to secure our homeland. The first order of business, when a country is invaded and thousands of her citizens are killed, is to shut down all movement into the country, take stock of what happened, and then move heaven and earth to ensure it does not happen again. Have you ever wondered why a border fence was not immediately erected? Have you ever wondered how—after it was discovered that many of the nineteen terrorists were on expired visas—no focused interior enforcement ever materialized? Have you ever wondered why the United States of America is still vulnerable to attacks through an open border and broken immigration system? Since 9/11, we have had two Republican and two Democrat presidents, and only one of these men was incorruptible and tried against all opposition from both parties to secure our great nation. It was not Bush or Obama, and it certainly wasn't Biden.

When Obama came into office, Border Patrol Agents held their collective breath, because we knew we would get no support. We knew Obama would never be a friend of ours, but we could have never expected what he would impose on immigration law enforcement officers. The Obama years were extremely dark times to be a Border Patrol Agent. President Obama engaged in criminal malfeasance by using prosecutorial discretion—which laid out guidelines on which illegal aliens were amendable to deportation—to shelter every illegal alien living in our country from deportation. This betrayal from Obama would be the genesis of what America is living through today under Biden.

It would be easier to detail who could be deported under the Obama guidelines than who could not. If an individual was a serial murderer or serial rapist, they might meet guidelines to be deported, but maybe not, as the US Attorneys would find loopholes for those animals. I can state that while I was a Supervisory Border Patrol Agent in an interior station in Orange County in Southern California, every illegal alien arrested under these oppressive guidelines was released. Illegal aliens who had already been deported, were violent criminals, and had exhausted all avenues of appeals were let go. President Obama effectively blocked any law enforcement action against the millions of illegal aliens living in our country. Even worse, a generation of Border Patrol Agents were frustrated, disillusioned, and broken. The highest-producing Agents simply shut down and engaged in no enforcement, and the average Agents did less than that.

Many Agents to this day claim that those years were the lowest and darkest times of the Border Patrol. Hope is the strongest emotion a human can possess, and there was no hope in the world of the Border Patrol. We felt like we had lost and there was no coming back. Our morale was eviscerated, and our great Border Patrol pride seemed to vanish. That was all about to change.

Enter the greatest president the Border Patrol could have ever wanted: Donald J. Trump. Everything seemed to change instantly. Hope was restored, because we knew we had a fighter for us—a man who ran his campaign on border security and American sovereignty. Trump was also not a politician and had no need for more money or more power; he had money and power in spades. In the beginning of his presidency, we wondered if he could fight off the vultures within his own party.

Paul Ryan and Mitch McConnell—leaders of the House and Senate—tried every tactic and constructed every obstacle they could to derail President Trump's desire to seal off the border. This is the perfect example of politicians from both parties ignoring the will of the people for their personal attainment of wealth and power.

President Trump knew the first step was to close and secure the border. He requested fifteen billion to build the border wall. The Republicans had control of both the House and Senate, and yet his own party would not fund this project needed to protect America.

Paul Ryan is an open borders advocate. Before he ran for Vice President with Presidential Candidate Romney—another open border advocate and slimy politician—a video had captured Paul Ryan and then Democratic Congressman Luis Gutierrez stating clearly that Ryan believed in not just amnesty or increased legal immigration, but open borders. When Paul Ryan began his failed campaign with Romney, strangely, I could not find that video anywhere.

Senate Majority Leader Mitch McConnell stonewalled Trump. Trump finally prevailed, but he only received $5 billion to build the wall. Stop for a second and remember that the same Republican party in both houses of Congress who were reluctant to fund $5 billion for America's protection have authorized and spent over $100 billion to fund Ukraine's border and over $1 trillion to help to secure Afghanistan and Iraq's sovereignty.

Trump's Wall! Credit: Dave Ellrod/EllrodImages.

President Trump did not stop with just the wall. He went further than any other President had ever done. He reached south into Mexico, Guatemala, Honduras, and El Salvador, and asked for help. The leaders of these countries were so used to dealing with the past presidents that had shallow and weak character that they told President Trump to pound sand. They miscalculated. Trump clearly stated that their defiance would not work and stopped all foreign aid to those countries. Since they are third world cesspools who desperately need American cash to function at all, they quickly changed their tune and did exactly what Trump demanded. He forced those countries to stand up their own Border Patrol and stop the flow of illegal aliens from crossing through the Northern Triangle countries leading to Mexico.

This significantly stopped the illegal flow of individuals into America. By 2019, for the first time in my twenty-four-year career, the Border Patrol was winning. Morale was off the charts. Pride throughout all ranks was back. Illegal aliens crossing the border knew that when they were arrested they were going straight back to their homeland. Illegal aliens living in the interior of the United States knew that no relief was going to be given once arrested, and they too were going to be deported. Several countries refused to take back their countrymen who were hardened criminals—why not, since the past weak and corrupted administrations had bent a knee to these nations? Not Trump. Trump knew he had power and flexed it. He used the same tactic he used against the Central American countries and Mexico: either accede to my demands or lose all foreign aid. Suddenly, ICE had flights scheduled across the globe to deport criminal aliens, who in prior presidencies would have been released onto our streets to terrorize our brothers and sisters.

By 2020, our twenty-four-hour daily arrest and getaway reports across the nation were shocking. The numbers on the two-thousand-mile southern border for arrests were nominal at best. In a twenty-four-hour period, we would arrest one hundred fifty to five hundred individuals! Again, that was over a twenty-four-hour period and across two thousand border miles. This report also showed a hundred or two hundred getaways, which the Border Patrol hated and diligently tried to get to zero. ICE Officers were arresting these getaways and criminal aliens in record numbers. Every Border Patrol Agent, from the new trainee to our Chief Rodney Scott, and ICE Officers throughout the ranks, believed we were on the verge of sealing the border and knew that we were putting a huge dent into the number of illegal aliens living in our communities, as their criminal alien arrests and deportations skyrocketed. Heading into the Presidential election in 2020, the Border Patrol knew that another four-year Trump presidency would mean an increasing success the Border Patrol could only have dreamed of decades ago. We had a president who had our back—who forced countries that only a few years before were abusing our borders and had laughed at us for decades to participate in ending illegal entries. Now these same disrespectful countries stood at the ready for our demands and obeyed. The Border Patrol and America had a president who understood the urgency to secure our borders and the significance of reclaiming our great nation's sovereignty, a president who could not be corrupted by money, because he had more money than the corruptors and therefore his own power. This made the elites and politicians confused, angry and vengeful.

On January 20, 2021, it all ended.

CHAPTER 4
Mayorkas

DEPARTMENT OF HOMELAND Security Secretary Alejandro Mayorkas is the tip of the spear on every decision causing the invasion on our borders.

Mayorkas did not begin his reign of eliminating immigration laws and policies when President Biden hired him to assume control over the largest law enforcement department in the nation. Mayorkas's America-last policies began during Obama's first term when Mayorkas was appointed the position of Director of US Citizenship and Immigration Services (USCIS). This was an extremely important position for Mayorkas. As Director of USCIS, he gained knowledge of the inter-workings of a powerful piece of the immigration engine. In his new position, Mayorkas went to work quickly as he was responsible for the creation and implementation of Deferred Action for Childhood Arrivals (DACA).

DACA is a boondoggle. In my extensive experience and research, every immigration policy creation, policy change, or newly crafted law has a nefarious angle built in. Never are these policies and laws created to help Americans; instead, they always lean strongly to the benefit of foreigners. Here are the base rules for DACA: You must be thirty-one years of age as of June 15, 2012, have entered the US before you turned sixteen years of age, and you must have lived continuously in the US since June 15, 2007. The explanation for the need for DACA is that children who illegally entered the United States as minors were brought to America as non-consenting adults and, therefore, should not be punished with deportation.

DACA sounds very fair and humanitarian until you peel off the first layer of another nefarious immigration law. First, who and how are we going to determine an illegal alien's age? Approximately three quarters of all migrant children that were arrested then placed with Health and Human Services (HHS) are between fifteen and seventeen years of age.[12] A large percentage of these "minors" are young adult men posing as children. Remember, almost all these unaccompanied minors do not come to America with birth certificates. Many times, throughout my career, these individuals had no idea what date they were born or how old they were. After making an arrest of an illegal alien, I would ask this individual for their biographical data. My second question after asking for their name was, "What date were you born?" I lost count of the number of times the response was, "Friday." I know that sounds unbelievable as citizens of a first world nation, but we are talking about individuals that are coming from poverty and chaos we can't fathom. Because of the change in detention policies for minors, these young adult men knowingly lie about their age and claim to be a minor so that they will be released. Secondly, how can a law enforcement officer determine if an individual did or did not reside continuously in the US for a specific time? ICE and Border Patrol are transporting, processing, and then finalizing the end of the smuggling event; so again, who is going to certify or dispute the claims made by individuals that have been coached on exactly what to say when being interviewed?

These laws are complex, and we know there is no one within the agencies who can or will do the needed investigations. Remember, we are now talking about an average of nine thousand individuals that give themselves up or are arrested daily. The chaos and overwhelming numbers of people is intentional, and it is working.

DACA law has been up and down the court system. DACA was recently found to be unlawful by the courts, but Biden and Mayorkas consistently work around the constitutionality of the court orders. It must be stated that one of Biden's first decisions as President was an Executive Order reinstating DACA. On his *first day* in office. There is a laundry list of problems with DACA. FAIRus.org does an incredible job of researching all aspects of immigration and their research of DACA is exceptional.[13] FAIR (Federation for American Immigration Reform) states that the overwhelming majority of DACA recipients average between the ages of twenty-seven and forty years old. Obama rubberstamped 98–99 percent of all DACA claims with minimal background checks. DACA is a major driver of the "family unit" invasion we are witnessing today on the border. These "family units" are used as shields against deportation because under current DHS policy, we will not separate family units. Prior to the DACA law in place under Obama and driven by Mayorkas, single adult males were the primary illegal crossers. Immediately after DACA was passed, an explosion of family units and Unaccompanied Alien Children (UAC) reached a crisis level.

DACA is no different than past immigration policies and laws in terms of the benefit gained by America, minimal to zero. Twenty-four percent of DACA recipients are functionally illiterate in the English language, only 46 percent have basic English skills, and only 49 percent have a high school degree. That doesn't sound like a net positive for America.

While in the powerful position of Director of USCIS, Mayorkas was a strong advocate of EB-5 visas. An EB-5 visa allows legal entrance to America if you will invest five hundred thousand dollars in a new business in the United States. Again, that sounds fair, but wait: this immigration law is also rotting with corruption, and Mayorkas found himself mired in it. EB-5 visas are notorious for fraud and abuse. As all elites believe they are above the law and being in a position of power, as Mayorkas was, favors to other elites like the Clintons, former Virginia Governor Terry McAuliffe, and former Senate Leader Harry Reid are expected.[14] Mayorkas pressured subordinates into securing EB-5 visas for the above-mentioned elites and their acquaintances. The Inspector General investigated and found no criminal acts but found numerous incidents of Mayorkas using his position to strongly influence subordinates to approve EB-5 visas to other powerful individuals *after* the visa applications were initially denied and even *after* denial in appeal.

Mayorkas moved from the Director of USCIS to the Deputy Secretary of DHS under President Obama. I remember this period in my career as a dark time. Under President Obama, with the guidance of Deputy Secretary Mayorkas, the Border Patrol was neutered. DHS instituted insanely high criminal prosecutorial guidelines for the US Attorneys for determining acceptance of a criminal referral and the determination of deportation of illegal aliens in the United States. Border Patrol

Agents would arrest hard core felons, sexual predators, and even prior deported illegal aliens with further deportation orders in the interior of the country—and we released them *all!* It is hard to articulate how maddening it was that almost every single illegal alien the Border Patrol or ICE Officers encountered in the interior was considered untouchable. This policy was an intentional bastardization of immigration law. You had top DHS leaders, like Mayorkas, that swore an oath to protect the American homeland erasing all immigration enforcement. I was a Supervisor at this time, and I watched every single one of my top producers stop working because they did not want to participate in the criminal orders handed down from above.

Just on the surface of Mayorkas's career we have DACA and the elimination of all interior law enforcement. Do you see a pattern beginning to materialize?

President Trump won the presidency, fired all the top brass that had corrupted the DHS, reversed numerous policies that harmed America and instituted strong immigration enforcement. For the first time in my long-suffering career, we, the Border Patrol, were finally winning. It was an incredible time to be a Border Patrol Agent!

Mayorkas was no longer welcome in an America-first government, so he went back to the private sector and waited patiently and with hope that another America-last president would take power.

Strong immigration law enforcement advocates watched in horror as the soon to be worst border president ever took office in 2021. President Biden appointed Mayorkas as the new Secretary of the Department of Homeland Security. Biden immediately fired off endless Presidential Executive Orders nullifying all the work the Border Patrol did the prior four years.

Mayorkas did not waste time. He reinstituted DACA, tried to void the Migrant Protection Protocols, tried to remove Title 42, and discarded every successful law enforcement strategy. I sat in my office as new DHS directives began to pour down to the ground level. I knew we were in trouble. However, nothing prepared me for what was to come.

From the moment Biden took office and Mayorkas took the reins of DHS, law enforcement operations died quickly. We immediately experienced sharp increases in arrests, getaways, and large caravans coming together south of the border. Our holding facilities across the border and in interior ICE facilities were instantly at maximum capacity. This was at the height of COVID, and we were ordered to do the unthinkable—release everyone! Every memo that we received at the station level from Sector HQ, which they received from Border Patrol HQ in D.C., was adversarial to our mission to secure our nation's borders. Unfortunately, this was just the beginning of lies, deception, and chaos.

Mayorkas in an intelligent man with an impressive resume starting with his education, his rise in the US Attorney ranks, and his rise into high powered political appointed positions. I do not question his ability or intelligence, because what he has accomplished in the intentional destruction of the American immigration system has been cunning, malicious, and strategically thought out and planned. What I dispute and argue against is his purposeful and destructive policies. His refusal to secure the border. There has not been one single law enforcement strategy to stop the continued invasion of illegal aliens into our country. Mayorkas has lied under oath to the House Judiciary Congress in May of 2022 when he defiantly stated that the border was secure: "The border is secure and we're executing our plan."[15] When he made that statement, the most recent monthly numbers were from March 2022 and showed over two hundred thousand illegal aliens were arrested and at least double that number made getaways. This statement was not a one-off or a mistake. Mayorkas has lied about it all. In two years as the Secretary of DHS, he has overseen approximately six million arrests and millions of getaways. As I wrote above, Mayorkas is an intelligent man. He is not incompetent or prone to make mistakes repeatedly. No. Mayorkas is deliberate in his decisions to undermine the nation's immigration laws. During a Congressional hearing in 2022, Congressman Ken Buck stated plainly to Mayorkas, "Many of my constituents have asked whether you will be impeached when Republicans gain control next year. They don't believe that you've committed a high crime, and they don't believe you've committed a misdemeanor. My constituents want you impeached because they believe you've committed treason. They believe you're a traitor. They compare you to Benedict Arnold."[16]

Congressman Buck's constituents have a point.

Mayorkas has an unbelievable ability to lie directly to Congress and make statements that are devoid of reality. In a Senate Judiciary Committee hearing in March 2023, Mayorkas was struggling to convince anyone that his abuse of the parole and asylum systems was securing the border. In one of his many famous quotes, Louisiana Senator John Kennedy stated, "Did you just parachute in from another planet, Mr. Secretary? Because you're the only person in the Milky Way who believes that we're not having massive, massive illegal immigration into America."[17] In one brilliant statement by Senator Kennedy, he was able to capsulize the complete picture of how Mayorkas's mind works. Senator Kennedy, like me, knows that Mayorkas is an accomplished and intelligent man. I honestly believe Mayorkas believes what he is doing is correct and maybe even noble, for he must believe that America has no claim on sovereignty and that all that America has is open for the taking. However, I could care less what this man believes or why he believes it. I know what he has done and continues to sustain is unconstitutional. Everything he has done is calculated.

In this same article, Senator Mike Lee from Utah echoes my point, "If the asylum process were followed—by the law—you would turn people away [and] you would send them back once you ran out of detention [space]. At the end of the day, it appears to me that you are not enforcing the law. You are redefining key statutory terms in order to obfuscate the fact that you're not enforcing the law. This is a fireable offense." Senator Ted Cruz from Texas followed up with, "Your refusal to do your job is revolting."

Words are powerful and if you listen to what people say, you do not have to guess what their true feelings are. This is true in what Mayorkas's response was to these powerful accusations from United States Senators by insisting that the immigration laws are "broken," rather than unenforced: "Unfortunately, our immigration system is not well designed to address the [investors'] need for labor [and] it is our hope that reform actually is legislated to address that issue." Look at what his response was to being called a Benedict Arnold and that his performance as Secretary was "revolting;" he cares about flooding America with more unskilled labor to help "investors." The border is wide open. Deadly narcotics are crossing into America by the tons daily, millions of illegal aliens have poured into our country, and no law enforcement measures are being enacted to stop this invasion. What this man wants to talk about is the need for investors to have more workers!

Mayorkas has taken the seeds of ongoing dysfunction and lawlessness from the Obama years and has propelled those unconstitutional ideals to depths of corruption in immigration that I never thought possible. In April 2023, Mayorkas has now ordered all Venezuelans arrested in Texas Border Patrol Sectors of Del Rio and El Paso to be placed in CBP detention facilities to await their asylum cases. Mayorkas has expelled Title 42 in those Texas sectors, two of the busiest sectors on the southern border.[18] CBP sources state the obvious, that detention space will fill to capacity overnight which will trigger Border Patrol to simply release every single Venezuelan. I promise you that every Venezuelan on the border is making their way to Texas right now. DHS put out this statement:

> Effective immediately, Venezuelans who enter the United States between ports of entry, without authorization, will be returned to Mexico. At the same time, the United States and Mexico are reinforcing their coordinated enforcement operations to target human smuggling organizations and bring them to justice. That campaign will include new migration checkpoints, additional resources and personnel, joint targeting of human smuggling organizations, and expanded information sharing related to transit nodes, hotels, stash houses, and staging locations. The United States is also planning to offer additional security assistance to support

regional partners to address the migration challenges in the Darién Gap.

I included that public information memo from DHS for two reasons: First, DHS distorts the truth of what is occurring with Venezuelans on the border. As if Venezuelans will choose to cross illegally outside of those two mentioned sectors in Texas. In this same statement, DHS makes the claim that they are working diligently to combat human smuggling. That is an absurd claim. Every one of the illegal aliens that cross the border are smuggled. The cartels own every piece of the border. No one crosses without paying for that privilege. Every illegal alien that crosses is told when, where, and what to do after they cross. It is all orchestrated to allow the cartels to move more narcotics safely. To make that claim that the DHS is working on combating human smuggling is ridiculous as over twelve to fifteen million illegals have already been smuggled in since Biden took office. The most important part of this statement that I want to focus on is the end: "…address the migration challenges in the Darién Gap."

The Darién Gap is on the southern end of Panama. It is the choke point of the trek north from South America. The Darién Gap is a violent place with difficult to traverse jungle terrain. Because the Darién Gap is a bottleneck location, the savages come to prey on these people like a fisherman shooting fish in a barrel. This is also a place where large migrant camps exist. These camps are a vital part of an attempted successful trek to America. Per the Council of Foreign Relations website, over one hundred and fifty thousand migrants went through these migrant camps from January to September 2022.[19] The numbers have steadily increased, which is a long way from a decade ago when the number of people making this trek was in the hundreds. The Darién Gap is a strategic location where the United States could put pressure on Panama to stop the hordes of humanity. Not our government. A former Green Beret and Special Forces veteran and now a photojournalist, Michael Yon, traveled to the Darién Gap with Congressmen Tom Tiffany (WI) and Burgess Owens (UT), deep into the jungle to witness the Darién Gap migrant camps. When they arrived in April 2022, they found Mayorkas and his security detail there as well. Yon claims that he not only has witnesses to Mayorkas being there, he also took drone footage of Mayorkas visiting the camps.[20]

With everything deteriorating on our border, why would Mayorkas be in the Darien Province of Panama? I will let Yon explain: "I had already been told by Senafront [*equivalent to the military and Border Patrol*] and the U.N. and some other people that the United States—Mayorkas—is coming down to increase the size of the camps—two of the camps—to double the size, which they did. I was droning. I droned when he was there. I droned this other camp. I've got all the drone footage, perfect HD." Mayorkas went to the Darién Gap migrant camps to increase their size in order to help facilitate a faster pace at which these migrants can travel to the US. Let that sink in for a second. Now tell me where my assessment of Mayorkas and his attempts at destroying America with unfettered immigration is wrong?

Yon states the truth when talking about who is funding and facilitating this treason: "The United States did this. Our Department of Homeland Security did it with our money. Our Department of Homeland Security is openly—they're not hiding it—it's in your face.... It's right there. They're breaking new ground as soon as [Mayorkas] left and increasing the size of the camps. It's unbelievable. They're well aware. It's our government that's doing it."

Many witnesses claim that thousands of people have died making the seven-day journey through the Darién Gap.[21] Yon stated plainly, "After being down there for months, and interviewing just tons of people—hundreds—I'm going to guess 10 percent die out there. And if 100,000 people came through this year, that's 10,000 people."

One year later in April 2023, things are so chaotic in the Darién Gap with migrant deaths, rapes, and other heinous crimes along with massive increases of illegal crossers, that Mayorkas was sent back down to Panama by the Biden administration to mitigate the issues in the migrant camps. Mayorkas and the countries of Panama and Columbia participated in a Trilateral Joint Statement claiming that all parties would work to shut down this migrant corridor. In typical Biden and Mayorkas fashion, all is not as it seems as part of this agreement states that one of the goals is, "Open new lawful and flexible pathways for tens of thousands of migrants and refugees as an alternative to irregular migration."[22] How about having one goal and that is stopping all migrants from coming into Panama to make their journey to the US? This Trilateral meeting reeks of Biden and Mayorkas covering their exposed asses. If the Biden administration is acting on the Darién Gap, I assure you the situation down there is beyond comprehension. The degradation and abuse must be shocking. The Panama-based Garry Conille, UNICEF Regional Director for Latin America and the Caribbean, might have discovered one of the reasons Mayorkas came running back down to the Darién Gap: "Our teams on the ground have never seen such numbers of children crossing the Panamanian jungle alone or with their parents."

What are the results of this expansion of these camps with US dollars prior to Biden's course correction? Panama claims a 450 percent increase of migrants traveling through the Darién Gap and these migrant camps to include a 3,000 percent of Chinese nationals.

The manifestation of these terrible and deliberate decisions by Mayorkas has led to a chaotic and unsustainable infrastructure of detaining and releasing millions of illegal aliens into America. A former colleague contacted me in April 2023 to tell me that his northern San Diego Border Patrol station and the other six San Diego Sector stations are so overcrowded that they are releasing everyone as quickly as they can. He also sent me a video filmed by Mexican narcotic cartel members driving on an interstate in Phoenix, Arizona. The two cartel members were driving through traffic with long rifles and several other firearms at the ready in case they were stopped by law enforcement. These two men were listening to Mexican music and talking about how weak the US government is. The cartels are here. They are staking claim to the southern border states, and they will move north. The cartels are emboldened, and why not? As much as it pains me to agree with those two cartel savages, our government is weak, impotent, and we don't have the will to stop them. In fact, our government's policies, and their refusal to enforce our laws will help these savages flourish in America.

Mayorkas has complete ownership of the following: DACA, prosecutorial discretion, abuse of asylum, abuse of immigration parole, stopping migrant protection protocols, undoing Title 42, catch and release, increasing the size of migrant camps in Panama, removing law enforcement posture, abusing EB-5 visas, unprecedented arrival of UACs and "losing" over eighty-five thousand UACs, creation of the CBP One App, releasing or not detecting between twelve and fifteen million illegal aliens into America. That list is incomplete and unfortunately growing.

After working under Mayorkas's rule, speaking with Border Patrol Agents on the ground, reading internal memos from DHS, and understanding the reasons why he changes and manipulates policy, I say this with complete confidence: Mayorkas is a traitor.

CHAPTER 5
How Did We Get Here?

THE COMPLETE DESTRUCTION of the American immigration system did not happen overnight. It has been a slow burn of lies, manipulation and collusion between both political parties and the elites that run our country who have been sabotaging our country since the fraudulent 1965 Immigration Act through unfettered immigration, useless amnesties, and now wide-open borders. In 1924, America saw the need to curtail legal immigration and the Immigration Act of 1924 (Johnson-Reed Act) was passed by President Coolidge. This law established the United States Border Patrol. Historians are split on this Immigration Act of 1924 as one side claims xenophobia and the other side claims America needed a break from mass immigration and the lax assimilation causing our nation to balkanize.[23] Sounds a lot like today! As I read through articles describing the concerns from Americans and their political representatives of that time, the concerns are the same as today. The labor market was flooded with unskilled cheap labor, the disproportion of immigrants from nations that did not share our cultural norms, beliefs and ideals, and the balkanization of our nation by nationalities. The biggest effect of this law was that it allowed America to determine who can immigrate to our country.[24] The Johnson-Reed Act drastically cut legal immigration and put limits on immigrant nationalities to 2 percent of the total number of people of each nationality in the US and essentially stopped all immigration from Asia. It is always interesting as we look back through the lens of 2023 and wag our finger at the past and call it racist, xenophobic, and all the other vile names. However, name another nation that allowed unfettered immigration in 1924 and in present times and is a successful nation? Did Japan, whose citizens were affected by this 1924 law, allow then or presently allow anyone to enter into their country. Absolutely not! Russia? China? Mexico? Central American nations? African nations? The answer is no, they do not, and yet there are no cries of racism. Why is that? Maybe because outside the liberal mindset of most of the west, countries greatly value maintaining their culture, language, customs, and wellbeing of their citizens. The idea that America must open its doors to the rest of the world is insane. This insanity continues to the present day. The idea that Americans must change their cultural and societal norms to conform to foreigners is a mental illness. America is the greatest superpower in all of history. This did not happen overnight. We became great because every person that entered our nation as a legal immigrant became an American, spoke English, adopted our culture, and agreed to live in our society under American norms. We are great because we are Americans, not because we have balkanized communities within a nation. My argument throughout this book is that America has a moral right to maintain America as she is and to become what Americans want her to become. America, through her political leaders who are our representatives, has a moral obligation to ensure her sovereignty and greatness. That is not achieved by diluting the value of American citizenship and flooding our nation with illegal aliens. America also has the moral high ground and moral authority to demand that if you come into our nation as a legal immigrant, you must assimilate and become an American. Why is that so controversial?

Assimilation is paramount to the success of any country that takes in immigrants. The assimilation of America's current immigrants and the millions of illegal aliens streaming into our towns, cities, and states is not happening.

Many in our country claim that this diversity is great for America. Somehow, speaking numerous languages, sharing no common ground on culture, and having no understanding of our nation's history or government is going to make America stronger. The truth is that this diversity is a rot in our country. The values that once unified our nation are now in decline. A recent poll in 2023 showed steep declines in what we now claim as American values.[25] The Wall Street Journal-NORC poll contrasted American values today compared to 1998. They found that the importance of patriotism dropped 32 percent. The importance of religion declined by 23 percentage points. Other areas of finance, work, and family also declined in importance. Does allowing millions of people from other countries to illegally enter America and that have no allegiance to the US play any role in this poll? American patriotism down by 32 percent! Diversity has made us divisive. The individuals making the diversity claim are ignorant pawns, but the elites and our political leaders know the rot is real and growing. Diversity to the political and elite class has a completely different meaning than it does to the average American. To the elites, diversity means separation and balkanization. To the average American, diversity means the convergence of ideas and life experiences that makes America great through the shared belief of what America is and what the responsibilities Americans must do to ensure our great nation continues.

Both legal and illegal immigrants left their homelands because they seek peace, opportunity, and freedom, all made possible by law and order. The irony is that the illegal aliens poured into our country against our law and created chaos instead of the order they desired. Name one aspect of the American way of life that is enhanced by more and more illegal aliens in our country. You can't name one, but you can rattle off an endless list of what negatively occurs due to their unlawful presence.

Great historians possess the ability to investigate a past historical event and work backwards to discover and articulate the causes of this event's success or failure. Historians will look at this current invasion of tens of millions of illegal aliens and work backwards to see the genesis of this great treason. The name that will pop up repeatedly in their investigations will be the late great "Lion of the Senate:" Ted Kennedy. Until his death, Senator Kennedy sponsored or cosponsored every immigration bill from the 1965 Immigration Act to the Immigration Reform and Control Act of 1986 (IRCA) that was Reagan's debacle of amnesty. Never discount the effect a single man can have on a nation. In the case of illegal immigration, Ted Kennedy was that man.

From 1924 to 1965, the majority of immigrants came from Europe, as did the pilgrims and our founding fathers. These immigrants were not allowed to walk into America and demand welfare or any other benefits. Instead, they had to prove that they would not become dependent on the government, needing any assistance to live in America. Shouldn't that simple fact of being self-reliant be paramount to becoming a legal immigrant? Do you think for a second Mexico would allow me to enter their nation as an immigrant and then need assistance to simply feed, clothe, and house myself? Many legal immigrants were sponsored by other family members to ensure that the newly arriving immigrant would not be a burden on society. Immigrants were turned away if they were sick, and this country demanded that they learn our language and customs as quickly as they could. My grandmother would tell me stories of how her family immigrated from Hungary and they never spoke their native tongue in order to learn English as quickly as they could.

Do you know that it is a deportable offense if a legal immigrant in 2023 takes any public assistance? Under the Immigration and Nationality Act (INA), a noncitizen is inadmissible if they are "likely at any time to become a public charge." Has Congress changed this law? No, they have not. So, why have Biden and the Department of Homeland Security Secretary Alejandro Mayorkas made being a legal immigrant dependent on government assistance *not* a deportable offense? Why?

The simple fact that millions and millions of immigrants, both legal and illegal, come to America annually, and only a handful of Americans leave, is the kryptonite to the left's insane claim that America is a racist and horrible place. Let me state right now that after decades patrolling the border, I witnessed tens of thousands of people climb the border fence and run north, sprinting to freedom. I *never* saw one person climb that same border fence and run into Mexico, not one.

Ted Kennedy brazenly stated that the 1965 Immigration Act—which he cosponsored—would not stop the flow of European immigrants, nor allow in untold numbers of individuals from the third-world countries of Africa and Latin America. Finally, he said, "The bill will not flood our cities with immigrants. It will not upset the ethnic mix of our society. It will not relax the standards of admission. It will not cause American workers to lose their jobs."[26] Take this infamous quote sentence by sentence and try to convince me that each statement was not a known lie. Every politician knew what was going to happen.

Of course, the "Lion of the Senate," along with most of Congress, convinced the late great conservative President Reagan to grant amnesty. To again prove my point that this betrayal of our country is a bipartisan affair, this boondoggle called the Immigration Reform and Control Act of 1986 (IRCA) was proposed by a Republican—Senator Alan Simpson from Wyoming. Reagan, through his presidency that spanned events like the fall of the Berlin Wall, several assassination attempts, his apology to America for lying about the Iran Contras, and afterwards to his death, repeatedly stated that agreeing to an amnesty was his greatest mistake.

The theme of every one of these amnesty pushes—from IRCA to amnesty for DREAMers (Children brought to America as minors) to the current call for amnesty—is that the system is overwhelmed, and the only answer is to purge it and start over. They claim that they will do better next time, but the next time is always the same. They intentionally break the system and then demand that the only answer is to let just a portion of the illegal aliens in our country be given amnesty. In 1986, they stated it would only be a million or so. The number grew to approximately three million. Today, the politicians scream for the DREAMers to receive amnesty and state there are only two million of these DREAMers. First, there is no such thing as "only" two million, and second, many of these "minors" are now in their twenties, thirties, and even forties.

Along came President Clinton and the passing of the Illegal Immigrant Reform and Immigrant Responsibility ACT (IIRIRA). Whenever the government uses words like Reform and Responsibility with Illegal Immigrant in an expanded title—run! I was hired as a Border Patrol Agent after this bill was passed. As with every previous bill, this one was destined to be a failure since these bills are created by politicians who never want to end the flow of illegal aliens or hold Americans accountable for hiring and exploiting them.

Think about this for a second. Do I need fancy words and titles to fix an issue that simple common sense would remedy? If I have a broken pipe in my house that caused my home to flood, do I stand in the water and throw my hands up? Do I call out to my neighbors, using confusing and irrational words and phrases? Do I walk away and ignore the flooding? Of course, the answer is: I turn off the water, remove the water in the house, find the broken pipe, and repair it.

The same applies to the border. It is that simple. Stop the flow of people pouring into our nation, remove the ones who absconded, find the holes on our border, then build and repair the broken fence.

Always remember that whenever the answer is simple, but politicians make the solution complicated and confusing, they are lying to you.

I remember learning a cold hard truth near the end of Clinton's presidency. I was driving north from the border on that dirty border street named Hollister, when I saw a man walking along the road. I was ending a midnight shift in a night of heavy fog, which meant a lot of getaways. This man looked back and saw my Border Patrol vehicle approaching him, but he did not try to run, nor did he look frightened at all. I got out of my vehicle ready to sprint, but the man just stood there as I walked up to him. As I was approaching him, he started to reach into his back pocket to pull out his wallet. I knew exactly what he was reaching for: the document that showed he was a citizen. Almost all of the people that live along the border carry their naturalization papers with them. We exchanged hellos as he began to unfold his naturalization certificate, and he stated that he had naturalized through President Clinton's immigration reforms. Then the lesson I would learn was uttered by this man in broken English: he wanted me to arrest every one of the illegal aliens living in his community, because they were taking away his jobs and reducing his wages. The irony was lost on the man that he was once an illegal alien doing the same destructive practices as the current illegal aliens in his community. The biggest irony is that every individual who becomes a citizen honestly and legally, or through fraud, is victimized by illegal aliens in lost wages, crime, and obtaining the American dream of freedom, opportunity, and order. The politicians that enact this insanity and the elites that champion these laws are never truly affected. They do not live in the barrios. They never have to compete for wages against someone who will do the job illegally for much less. They will rarely if ever suffer the pain of rape, murder, or theft. They live in a different world with protection and safety the majority of us will never know. How fast would the wall go up if these illegal aliens were lawyers, journalist, and politicians, instead of maids and landscapers? We all know the answer: immediately!

Then President Bush and 9/11 happened and our nation turned upside down. Patriotic Border Patrol Agents were chomping at the bit to do our jobs right, because we all believed that the nation had hit its collective limit to the decades of insane immigration policies and politicians ignoring the problem. We waited for our orders to enforce the immigration laws that we had all sworn an oath to enforce and defend. Those orders never came, and we did nothing different.

In fact, as an agency, we regressed. Agents became disillusioned and frustrated. One of my fondest memories of this bumbling word salad of a president was when he was asked about a great moment in his life. I remember reading his answer while I was on the border working—he stated that his fondest memory was working in the fields harvesting crops with Mexicans. Remember that this was a United States president, a minority owner of the Texas Rangers major league baseball team, someone who had traveled the world, and someone who had access to people, money, and power. And his greatest memory was working in the fields with Mexicans picking crops? How about something, anything, that would put an American in this story? You are the president of the most powerful nation in the history of the world, and this is what you pick. I remember reading this and knowing that I lived in a different world from these people. Stories like that confirmed my belief that America was run by elites who had more in common with a tree than their fellow citizens.

Then President Obama was elected president and the Border Patrol entered our darkest hours. He famously stated, "We will fundamentally transform the United States…." Well, if you love something, the last thing you would do would be to fundamentally transform it. Obama laid the foundation upon which President Biden would complete four years later. Obama forced Assistant United States Attorneys (AUSA) to use prosecutorial discretion when deciding if an illegal alien would face criminal charges for crimes committed in the US and if these same individuals would be deported. Obama's administration made these prosecutorial discretion guidelines so rigid that every illegal alien living in the United States was now immune from deportation, including violent felons, criminals of all sorts, and previously deported aliens. This only encouraged more illegal entries, because the thinking was, "If I can just make it past the Border Patrol and reside in America, I will be free until the next amnesty."

The millions of future illegal aliens were correct. As a Supervisory Border Patrol Agent, I watched as my best Agents shut down, refusing to patrol highways, public transportation, or other areas with high levels of illegal aliens. Why? Because every person who was arrested was eventually let go. I remember one day when one of the most productive Agents in the station looked up all his arrests from the previous two years and discovered that every single person he had arrested was released into America. He shut down that same day.

From 1965 to the present, the narrative stays the same, but the terms change. The narrative is simple and irrational once you peel back the first layer of nonsense. The chant goes like this: "We are a nation of immigrants. The diversity these people bring to our country makes us stronger. The immigrants work harder than Americans." And further: "These people are good family people, and they just want an opportunity and they, like us, deserve that opportunity."

I could write a book just on this false narrative, but I only have to scratch the surface to destroy it. First, we are not a random group of immigrants that stumbled upon a great nation. We are a nation of people that have spilled blood, lost treasure, and many died, creating the greatest nation on planet earth. We own it and we get a say to who enters. Secondly, diversity is not a strength. Our greatest strength is that Americans are Americans, and we share the same language and culture. Our beliefs align, and we would die for each other and for the country that provides the greatest quality of life in the world. Thirdly, if these immigrants worked harder and were smarter than us, then why are their countries so messed up that they bust through our borders to live here? Lastly, no one deserves our opportunities. We own these opportunities, and America and her citizens come first, always first!

The term has also changed over time, from "illegal alien"—a description used in courts of law—to "the undocumented." The term "illegal alien" is now considered so bigoted that my computer keeps underlining these words as hateful speech. We are told no human is illegal and that God does not like borders. Borders are now synonymous with hate, division, and white supremacy. The Left has hijacked the language and as always, the Republicans and many conservatives sit idly by. We now call illegal aliens of all ages DREAMers, as if this makes them soft and cuddly. Criminal aliens are just "oppressed people."

President Obama was a master at the manipulation of terms, and moving the narrative along the path that benefited him. Unlike his Democrat successor who is functionally incoherent, having no control over his thoughts and speech, President Obama was eloquent and smooth. He cast irrational beliefs as not only rational but necessary. At the time, we in the Border Patrol despised this man as he unraveled all our work.

It is human nature to believe during dark times that there will never be good days again. I learned again that good days were for sure coming again when President Trump was brought into office and, despite opposition from his own party, delivered sweeping change. For the first time in my career, illegal aliens feared being arrested and deported. Southern nations that for decades had abused our nation's sovereignty and kindness were now submissive to a leader who demanded respect and articulated expectations that if left unfulfilled would have severe consequences. Morale in all ranks of the Border Patrol was the highest I had ever seen. Pride that months earlier was nonexistent was now at the forefront of our agency.

Our Border Patrol Union backed Trump throughout his candidacy. I have worked for presidents who did not respect me or my agency, who undercut our presence and removed our authority, and I witnessed our own government do everything in its power to obstruct and handcuff us.

To this day, it is so difficult to wrap my mind around the fact that I swore an oath to protect America with the laws Congress passed, and yet the same Congress forbade me from enforcing their laws. This same Congress calls for the defunding of my agency. This same Congress calls me hateful names and accuses me and my colleagues of unfounded and ludicrous crimes. And yet this same Congress does not change one law on the books, because its legislators know deep down everything that they say is a lie.

By the end of Trump's presidency, the border was on the verge of being sealed shut, our immigration system was working, and the traitors within DHS were being located and removed.

Our Chief Rodney Scott was one of us and was aligned with President Trump. Agents believed that the future was unlimited and that all the pain, injuries, and betrayal were now all worth it. America was going to be safe, as law and order were now going to rule the land.

The immigration world was about to change for the worse. It would get so bad that most of my former colleagues, and my sources, believe that there is no coming back from this administration's treason. Treason is a harsh word, but it fits perfectly for this administration. If I described a government that welcomed and facilitated millions of people to enter into America illegally, removed all obstacles in immigration policy and laws to further increase illegal entries, stood the Border Patrol down and stopped all law enforcement functions, and then created new and unlawful policies out of thin air to again further the illegal entries of millions of people all the while not performing one law enforcement strategy, what would you call those people in the government? Everything I just wrote is happening in present time. Over five million individuals have crossed our borders illegally, most of them fraudulently granted asylum relief or Immigration Parole. The getaway numbers from DHS for the month of November 2022 shows over ninety-four thousand. I know from my experience and from talking to my sources that ninety-four thousand getaways is a complete lie. That monthly number is closer to three to five hundred thousand illegal aliens who have and are going to cross illegally into our country undetected.

There is no law enforcement strategy being proposed or implemented to stop this invasion. Instead, our own government is removing all impediments to a safe passage into

America. Biden and his team are using Border Patrol policies like Immigration Parole in ways never intended.

Biden announced in January of 2023 that he is opening thirty thousand more parole cases a month for citizens of Haiti, Cuba, Venezuela, Honduras, and Nicaragua.[27] *This is against the law!* Only Congress, not the Executive Branch, can determine how many and from which countries individuals can immigrate. My eleven-year-old son knows the different roles of the three branches of the government, but Senate and House Democrats are told to say nothing and remain loyal to the party. The media remains silent; journalists are all grossly ignorant, or they have skin in the game that they are protecting. Because our own government does not know the Constitution or does not care, this president forces the issue of unfettered immigration by stating, "I am left with only one choice—to act on my own, to do as much as I can on my own to try to change the atmosphere."[28] Nowhere in the Constitution does it say, "Hey, if the Congress doesn't want to do something, just do it yourself to change the atmosphere!" Mark Levin, the great constitutionalist and conservative radio host, nailed it when he stated, "We are living in a Post-Constitutional America."[29]

What should cause the greatest anxiety among our citizens is that both parties are in on this. Both political parties stand by this frail old man, all nodding in agreement with Biden when he makes these blatantly unconstitutional statements. For God's sake, all any politicians—Democrat or Republican—have to do is stand up, hold the Constitution in their hand, and say, "Hold on! You can't do this because the Constitution is clear on your authority." But they won't stand up and speak the truth, so the citizens of our great nation must understand that there is a reason why our leaders refuse to comply with the laws of our nation, although that reason is hard to swallow. They don't care what the laws are because they think those laws do not pertain to them, and their greed for more wealth and power is more important than our constitutional republic.

I am often asked the question, "Can we make it back from this?" My answer is, "I don't think so," because the only way to reverse what has taken place for almost six decades, especially with the accelerated pace of the last two years, is for a strong leader to make sweeping changes that the power structure will fight with everything it has. This leader would have to remove, through force if necessary, all illegal aliens from our country, and seal the border once and for all.

Who is that leader? I think it is Trump. I can state with absolute confidence that if Trump was still president none of what is happening now would have ever occurred. Instead, the border wall would have been completed and fortified. ICE arrests would have continued to climb as illegal aliens in the interior would have been located and deported. I pray for such a leader and for men to stand strong beside this leader. It can be done, but will it happen? I do not know.

CHAPTER 6
Show Us Respect! We Demand it!

IT IS MIDNIGHT and the pouring rain floods the polluted Tijuana River, causing it to swell past its banks. It's January and the wind off the Pacific Ocean makes it seem colder than the temperature actually is. The whole west side of the Imperial Beach Station's AOR is flooded, and the only vehicles that can snake through the maze of small rivers that were once smuggling trails is the ATV Unit. Me and my ten ATV riders have our Border Patrol rain slickers on, but we are all soaked to the bone as our shift comes to an end. My men and I have been soaking wet for ten hours, and as we ride our ATVs in this weather it feels as if we are all naked. The rain hits the parts of our faces not covered by our helmets and goggles, and the cold wet wind pushes against our bodies. My feet squish inside my black leather boots and I can feel the wetness on my body despite multiple layers of clothes underneath my Border Patrol uniform.

We are driving in a single file line on the blacktop of Monument Road as our shift ends. As we turn onto Hollister

Street and begin to head north back to the station, with the border now at our backs, the radio crackles in our earpieces as the East Scope Operator calls out a large group of seventeen bodies running from the north side of the Tijuana River to the levee. The shift is not over after all.

Swing Shift ATV Unit—HEROES!

I have worked alongside some of the most impressive people in some of the worst environments. These people, my Border Patrol partners, never complained, but instead just did their job in the face of daunting challenges that would force a weaker person to run for the hills. I worked with patriotic veterans that served for years in the Army, Marine Corps, Air Force, and Navy. The atmosphere in the Border Patrol has always been, "Just get it done!" We have for decades completed our mission without the funding or the backing from our political leaders. I have worked with and watched Border Patrol Agents fight back resentment and anger from the vile names we are called by activists and by our government. Despite this betrayal from our government, Border Patrol Agents fight side by side with their partners as we have felt alone in this world of immigration. We fight for America, but in the day-to-day physical battles with our enemies, we fight solely for each other.

Within the Imperial Beach's AOR is a sewage treatment plant that the US paid for, but its sole operation is to handle Mexican sewage and waste. During the construction of this 186-million-dollar project paid by us for Mexico, the construction company would do enormous amounts of earth moving throughout the day and then place small caution flags around trenches they had just cut open. For Agents working on ATVs, this was an accident waiting to happen. The night had fallen and just like in the movies, everything bad starts to move around in the darkness. The last thing I remember from that night, as I woke up in the hospital with a broken shoulder, was the sun disappearing and the sounds of dispatch calling out sensor activations. The accident report stated that I had responded to a sensor hit and a scope operator calling out bodies moving north from The Fingers—three hills that ran south to north from the border with deep canyons on the east side, causing them to look like fingers. Once the illegal aliens dropped into The Fingers, they had a direct shot at crossing Monument Road, which paralleled the border fence. Once they made it north of Monument Road and into the thick trees and dense brush, the odds increased in their favor.

I was driving my ATV hard and fast south, then west, along a dirt road just north of Monument Road, trying to get in front of this group. However, earlier in the day the construction crew had cut a deep, fifteen-to-twenty-foot-wide trench across this dirt road, which had caused the dirt road to form a ramp on either side of the trench. When I came around the corner on this dirt road and began to straighten out, I hit that ramp that wasn't supposed to be there at about fifty miles an hour. I must have hit the brakes at the last second, causing me to slow down a little and not able to clear the trench. I took flight and my ATV slammed into the other side of the trench, crushing it like an accordion. I slammed into my ATV, and the wall of dirt knocked me out and destroyed my shoulder. I recovered as quickly as I could, and after two months, I got back on another ATV and rejoined my brothers.

I still can't sleep on that side of my body after fifteen years, causing me to toss and turn throughout the night.

When I think about my time on the border working with my friends, I have great pride in what we accomplished. We left it all on the field of play. I left a part of my body and heart on that border. Many times, certain areas or exact spots have been named after an Agent. I was honored when that dip in the earth was named "J. J.'s Dip". Agents still reference "J. J.'s Dip" when they call out their location, or where alien traffic has gone through. I take great pride that I own that small piece of the border.

I was a Supervisor of my own ATV Unit, and I loved it. The ten agents who worked for me in this unit worked like a pack of wolves. The Tijuana–San Diego border was the most violent section of the border in recent history. We had bricks and concrete with rebar protruding out of it thrown at us, many times striking us as we drove our ATVs. One of my guys and I were driving slowly along the border fence cutting the dirt road for footprints. All of a sudden, I saw a smuggler rise up on top of the fifteen feet high fence, lifting a solid piece of broken concrete over his head. I couldn't call out quickly enough, as the smuggler threw that block of broken concrete right at my buddy, hitting him square in his chest, causing him to violently fly off his ATV and strike the ground.

When I retired from the Border Patrol in July of 2021, I forced myself to disengage from anything about the border. I moved my family to South Dakota, where our lives could slow down and simplify, where we could raise our son in a community that shared our values, since sharing common values was no longer working in California. When my wife and I watched the news and a border story came on, I would either turn it off or walk into another room. When I spoke with my former colleagues and friends, I would ask them not to talk to me about the border or the job. I would swipe by all stories on the internet about the Border Patrol and immigration. I was successful for about eight months, then—as Biden's intentional destruction of the border increased—news organizations I had been in contact with prior to my retirement tracked me down. I was pulled back into the fray, but I was rested and ready to go. I quickly found myself on Fox and Friends, *NewsMax*, radio shows, and podcasts. I read and listened to the talking heads on cable news and watched the endless videos of hundreds of illegal aliens wading across the Rio Grande, but that wasn't the whole truth. I knew that I had the whole truth: I possessed information from experience and numerous sources about what was happening, how it was happening, and why. I had to get back into the fight, because although I may not wear that green uniform any longer, I am still a Border Patrol Agent.

Prior to my retirement and under the leadership of President Trump, we had a strong national Border Patrol Chief: Rodney Scott. He was all about securing the border and thinking outside the box, but always relying on boots on the ground as the best defense. For the first time in a long and defeated career, the organizational alignment from the President through DHS to our Chief, down to the sectors and stations, allowed for immediate success, strength, and commitment throughout the rank and file. I spoke regularly with my ICE friends, and they were tearing it up. They focused on the criminals, but if they came across anyone illegal, they would arrest that person. Illegal aliens knew if they crossed the border and were arrested, we would give them no relief; they were deported immediately. If they came from a land far away, a plane was waiting to take them back. Illegal aliens who once lived without fear of being located in the interior of the United States were now living in fear of being found and deported.

The actual immigration system worked. The badly kept secret is, there is no need for more immigration laws, because what is on the books works. Yes, there needs to be a review and tightening of all policy and law, but if the law as now written is enforced correctly, we can get back to those winning days.

I have witnessed the wear and tear of an Agent's body over time. The career of any law enforcement officer is difficult, particularly in immigration law enforcement. Bad backs, broken bones and bad knees are what hard working Agents look forward to as they age. The endless shifts of tracking illegal aliens up and over mountains, wading across rivers, and running down dark trails in the pitch dark, the pain from just wearing a gun belt for decades—all has a profound effect on Agents over a twenty-five-year career. I have seen a friend's head caved in from a large rock thrown at him, and I have witnessed one of my ATV riders hit a concrete pylon, severing his pinky finger from his hand except for one tendon that saved it from falling onto the dirty border. I have also been to the funeral of an Agent who took his own life.

The cold detached reaction you develop to the horror of life is part of the job, and you accept it as just as it is. But what Border Patrol Agents can't stomach, what causes them great angst, is the utter lies told about them from the very people who are supposed to be their leaders.

For example, President Biden and his Border Czar Kamala Harris lied to America that the Horse Patrol Unit in Texas was whipping illegal aliens from their horses with whips. It was all a lie. If you have ever ridden a horse, you can imagine trying to control a beast weighing two thousand pounds as people are running around and under that large animal. The fact that several illegal aliens were not trampled and killed is a miracle. Those Horse Patrol Agents should have been given citations of courage and excellence in controlling the obviously chaotic situation. However, this is a perfect example of the distortion of the truth by our very own leaders without a single thought about the turmoil that will befall the Agents. As of this writing, those poor Agents are still under some form of investigation *after* they were found to be not guilty of this false accusation. And President Biden, Harris, and their administration continue to sell the lie that Agents were whipping illegal aliens.

We all mightily try to compartmentalize our anger and resentment away from our responsibility to do our job. But it is extremely difficult to lie in a hospital bed with broken bones from wrecking your vehicle as you pursue a Failure to Yield human smuggling load or watch as your brother or sister is killed in the line of duty while our leaders demonize us. We are slandered as Nazis who use Nazi tactics. The truth is, I could do the politician's job with my eyes closed, and I would do it better than they do (not by lying to and stealing from America, but by using that position of power to lead our country to greatness). However, none of those pansy-assed, soft, weak politicians could ever do even the most menial task of a Border Patrol Agent. They could never walk through the dark wooded areas of the border knowing large numbers of illegal aliens were walking that same trail and that they were going to meet them shortly. Those same politicians could never fight and win a struggle with a hardened violent criminal. Those politicians would faint at the sight of a MS13 El Salvadorian gangbanger in a hollowed out hootch at three o'clock in the morning, where it would be just them and that savage.

Let me tell you a story that best describes the work of a Border Patrol Agent. I told this story for the first time at my retirement party, because I wanted to remind the Agents in attendance that not everyone can do our job. In fact, only a very few can.

My dad was larger than life to me. Most young kids think their dad is a bad and tough dude. Well, that wasn't true for almost all of my friends, but it was true for me, and all my friends knew it. My dad was a huge man standing at six feet four and 275 pounds. He had jet-black hair and very dark tanned skin. Many people thought he was Italian, but he wasn't Italian—he was Hungarian and Blackfeet Indian. He looked the part of a hitman; he had huge hands and arms, and his dark complexion and towering stature was intimidating to everyone including my friends and their fathers. However, he loved to laugh and tell stories and was a great husband and a loving father who showered his six children with unconditional love. In short, he was an awesome dad. We were all so proud of him and the accomplishments he earned throughout his career as a Special Agent in Charge in the Secret Service.

I was still a young Agent with about five years in the Patrol, and my parents flew out to San Diego to visit me. My dad loved that I was in the Border Patrol, and he asked if he could go on a ride-along with me. I was excited to show my dad what I did because I wanted his approval. He always gave me love and support, but I always wanted to make him proud of me as well. I brought him to our swing shift muster, introduced him to my unit, and told them about his career in the Secret Service. I will always remember how proud I was when they stood up and gave my dad a standing ovation. My Supervisor gave me an all-shift backup position so I could respond to all traffic that crossed into our AOR. I grabbed my keys and my father, and I took off toward the border. I worked swing shift because the hours were great for me. I could spend half the shift tracking out any gotaways north of the border from the day shift then I could prepare myself for nightfall as the border would come alive. I always compared working the border at night as playing hide and seek with a gun and pending violence. My dad and I responded to several arrests, and he got to see what type of person we arrested in Imperial Beach—almost exclusively criminals. The sun began to set and the darkness of the night fell upon us. The border changes at night: it gets strangely quiet and the wet night air and fog change the mood. My dad, being a federal law enforcement agent himself, instantly recognized the change and tone of the moment. Our conversations became more serious, and he understood the game had changed.

We were driving around north of the Tijuana River, near a baseball field just south of a border neighborhood, and we could see the fog settling in over the Tijuana River. We stopped and parked near the baseball field facing south to the border and we could see the orange haze from the border lights cascading down on the hills. I was telling my dad about this area, and how I had arrested several groups coming out of the Tijuana River, when my vehicle radio blasted out a call from an Agent that was tracking a group to our west, "This is India 330. I have a group of seven to ten making their way from the 90s traveling east. I am following them and the sign [footprints in the sandy trails] are heading to Hollister Bridge." I looked at my dad and told him that that group was heading right toward us. I grabbed the vehicle's radio mike, "10-4, I'm north of The Ghost Trail. I will walk in and lay up." I looked at my dad and said, "Let's go!"

As we started to walk from the baseball fields to the entrance of The Ghost Trail, I saw that my dad was acting a little strange, but I let it go as I was focused on getting in place to make this arrest. The Ghost Trail is a narrow dirt path that smugglers use once they cross over or around the Tijuana River. The Ghost Trail also looks like a scene out of a horror movie. On either side of the dirt path is dense brush and overhanging trees closing off any light from the moon. When it is foggy, it is pitch black inside this trail. When it is cold out and you can see your breath, along with the landscape and the pending confrontation with criminals, this place becomes haunting.

My dad and I were getting closer to the entrance of The Ghost Trail, and about fifty feet away he grabbed my arm and stopped me. I am a big guy, and even though my dad was in his sixties, he seemed to tower over me. He looked down at me and then turned and pointed to the black hole that was the entrance to The Ghost Trail and said with his big booming voice, "J. J., aren't you going to turn on your flashlight?" Whispering, I responded, "Shhh, they might hear us. No, Dad, if I turn on my flashlight, they will know we are here." I tried to turn toward the black hole, but he again grabbed my arm, stopping me, and loudly said, "Wait! So, you are telling me that there are seven to ten men walking inside there, and you are not going to turn on your flashlight?" Before I could answer, he continued, "And there is no one coming to help you?" I replied, "No Dad, it's just me. You will need to stay right behind me, and I will take care of everything." My dad became angry, and I will never forget his words, "No! No! No! This is fucking crazy! Take me back to your truck!"

We hurriedly walked back to my truck as I snuck quick looks at him. I could not believe that my huge dad, who was ready to take a bullet for United States presidents, would not walk into The Ghost Trail and do what I had been doing for five years. I got him safely in the truck, ran back to The Ghost Trail, and waited for the group to come to me. As I waited in that dark trail, I smiled as pride coursed through me, because the man I admired the most thought what I did for a living was crazy—too crazy even for him. I knew at that moment that what I did for a living was unique and special: being a Border Patrol Agent took courage and determination.

I took my dad home that night, and he was particularly quiet. I woke up the next morning to find my mom in the kitchen making some breakfast, and I asked, "Where's Dad?" My mom smiled and said, "Your father is still sleeping." She paused, then continued, "Your father is so proud of you. He woke me up last night when you got home from work and he told me about your night together, 'Our son does a man's job. Only a real man can do what he does.'" Those words from my dad still fill me with pride.

This is what my dad and I saw looking at the border from north of The Ghost Trail, orange haze and fog.

There have been thousands and thousands of warriors like me that battled the enemy at our walls, against criminals that the average American would run in utter fear from. Not the Agents I worked with—we all stood tall and fought.

There is no other law enforcement organization that works in the environment that we do. There are no other agencies or departments that perform their law enforcement duties the way the Border Patrol does. There is no other law enforcement agency or department that is assaulted at the level we are. This job is not for the faint of heart, because the Border Patrol Agent's greatest enemy and fear is not the savage who was just released and deported for murder, or the savage that raped and brutalized young children—no, we fear and loathe the politicians and the traitors not only within our own government, but inside our own DHS. The real savages are the traitors who hurl vile names at the men and women doing what the politicians agreed upon and made into law.

One afternoon there was a radio call from our dispatch that a carjacking had just taken place, and the San Diego PD was involved in a high-speed chase that was coming to the border. Half of my ATV Unit was on the west side of Imperial Beach's AOR. As further reports stated that this "failure to yield" was exiting I-5 and heading south on Monument Road toward the border, my guys started moving east toward the fun. I was coming from a different location, and I was ahead of my unit when dispatch radioed that the stolen vehicle had crashed and rolled over just east of Hollister Street on Monument Road.

The San Diego Police requested back up. I was there within a minute. As I drove up on my ATV, I saw the vehicle on its side in the thick brush on the north side of the street, with its wheels still rotating and two San Diego police officers standing near the vehicle. I turned off my ATV and greeted the officers, assuming they had placed the bad guys under arrest. I was wrong. One of the officers said that two individuals had run away and up the hillside to the south. I pointed to the face of a hill that rises about a hundred feet high and asked if they had made it over the ridge and they said no. I stood there, kind of confused as to why they weren't running up that hill to find these criminals. I asked why they were standing with me instead of going up the hillside. They both said at once that they were waiting on the K-9 dogs. Just then, I could hear the noise of ATV engines coming closer to the crime scene. I turned to the police officers and said, "Here come *my* dogs." As they got closer, I radioed to them that two subjects had run up the face of Pink's Drive. Three ATVs roared past us and turned sharply onto a dirt road leading up Pink's Drive, then split off to cut the dirt roads that ran east to west trying to locate the bad guys' footprints on the sandy trails. In less than two minutes, my guys had found the two subjects hiding in high grass.

The three of us watched from afar as my guys handcuffed the two felons and laid them over the seats of two of their ATVs and—sitting on top of them—drove them down to the police officers. After putting the criminals in the police cruiser, both cops shook their heads at us and said, "Man, you guys are crazy." We all revved up our engines and, as we drove off, I smiled and yelled over the engine noise, "Yes, we are!"

Border Patrol Agents are a different breed of law enforcement, and we are proud of that! Instead of being demonized by politicians, elites, and civil rights groups, we should be praised, or, at the very least, thanked.

Imagine you are a firefighter and you responded to a five-alarm fire. You and your partners are running up and down the stairwell, saving men, women, and children. Now imagine the mayor and city leaders turn off the water to your hoses and throw huge dry logs into the building, and as you try in vain to save more people, you are screamed at that you are a racist and a coward. That is no different than what is happening daily to the men and women of the Border Patrol.

A simple thank you would be nice.

CHAPTER 7
Why?

WHY IS THIS happening? It is difficult to convince people why this crisis is occurring, because the reasons are so simple. Because the border and immigration issues are so deeply layered with fraud and corruption, people think the explanation for why the politicians and elites want this chaos must mirror the complexities of the problem. The reason why millions of illegal aliens are ushered into our nation is right in front of you: votes and wealth from complete demographic change.

The Democrats are driven by power, and the source of that power is votes. Illegal aliens, whether they obtain citizenship or don't, vote 99 percent Democrat. How fast would Senator Schumer and former House Speaker Pelosi build an impenetrable wall if these same illegal aliens would vote 99 percent Republican? We all know the answer to that: all the Democrats in unison would say exactly what I am writing in this book. They would be outraged and demand that every last illegal alien be deported, and the harshest fines be levied against American companies, large and small. You would hear old, bent-over Schumer with his hair plugs screaming about how the American worker's wages are being depressed and how the Republicans are all about big corporations making money. Nancy Pelosi, with her permanently raised eyebrows, would be banging her fist on the podium, shrieking about how the American voter is being disenfranchised and how America's sovereignty is at peril. The Democrats are all about the votes. They care not one bit about America and her citizens.

Another example of the Democrats' endless pursuit of power is that Democrat-run states and cities are allowing illegal aliens to vote in their state and local elections. If these illegal aliens voted Republican, do you believe this would be allowed? California, Vermont, Massachusetts, Illinois, Washington, DC, and New York either allow illegal aliens to vote, or are trying to pass legislation to allow it.[30] What do all these locations share in common? They all have large populations of illegal aliens, and they all have Democrat-controlled legislatures.

Allowing non-citizens to vote is injuring our Republic in numerous ways.

What makes America great is that the voice of the people is heard through the power of voting. Voting allows citizens to be heard and have a strong say in how their community and nation will be governed. Allowing millions of individuals who are not citizens to vote waters down the citizen's vote. Vermont Democrat State Representative Hal Colson—who sponsored one such bill to legalize illegal alien voting—said, "People always glom onto the idea that you have to earn our right to vote by becoming a citizen."[31] The right to vote is predicated on citizenship. Do you think the countries that help facilitate the crossing of millions of illegal aliens, Honduras, Guatemala, El Salvador, and Mexico, would ever allow non-citizens to vote in their elections? Would any country, even the worst-run countries on the planet, allow non-citizens to vote in their elections? The answer is absolutely not, and they don't!

Many Americans want to ignore what is happening because they either feel helpless against the power structure that is in place, or it is difficult for them to comprehend and acknowledge the idea that their country's government is so corrupt. The corruption within our government is so deep and so widespread it is impossible to trust anyone or any institution.

I have come to expect this behavior from Democrats in political office but where are the Republicans?

The Republicans are right beside the Democrats. Their driving motivation is also the attainment of more and more wealth. The purposeful creation of a black market of labor is solely for the benefit of the elites. The cheaper the labor, the more money made by corporations, which leads to more money via political contributions and future employment opportunities for the politicians. Have you ever wondered how I can order an expensive computer, a pair of socks, and a book from Amazon which delivers my items the next day, but our government claims that it is helpless in tracking who works legally in our country? When a chicken or a cow contracts a disease and the market is tainted, that same government that claims they can't find illegal aliens can locate the exact farm where that animal came from.

Our government has a process to determine who can legally work, receive social services, and receive medical services called eVerify, which can verify an individual's citizenship and rights to our government's services. Why isn't eVerify made mandatory in every state to receive social services, non-life threating medical services, or approve legal employment?

In 2016, the Republicans had control over the House, Senate, and presidency. They could have stopped all this insanity, created laws demanding the use of eVerify, built the wall, and deployed more and more resources to the border to seal it off. These measures would have stopped the flow of illegal aliens from crossing the border, and eVerfiy, coupled with stiff fines on employers, would have forced these illegal aliens to return to their homelands. Then, the Republicans could have streamlined and modernized the immigration system to work for our country and our citizens.

As much as I despise the political leaders on both sides of the aisle, I cannot believe that they are this functionally stupid and negligent. Instead, I know that these individuals follow the plan set in motion, fearful that if they step outside the groupthink or question the logic of unfettered immigration, they will pay a steep price from their party's leadership.

When once in a blue moon they are affected by their bad decisions, they freak out and show us their true beliefs. This recently happened three times in three different locations. First, buses of illegal aliens who were arrested on the southern border were driven to the cities of New York and Washington, DC—both sanctuary cities for illegal aliens. New York City ended up with approximately fifteen thousand illegal aliens. Mayor Adams freaked out. The mayor and his city that preached to the lowly southern border towns about compassion and kindness, demanded that this invasion stop. He stated that New York City could not handle so many illegal aliens: crime was spiking, and the schools could not accommodate so many non-English speaking students. Mayor Adams demanded billions of dollars in aid from the federal government, because, as he stated,

We are at our breaking point. Based off our projections, we anticipate being unable to continue sheltering arriving asylum seekers on our own and have submitted an emergency mutual aid request to the State of New York beginning this weekend. This type of request, reserved only for dire emergencies, asks the state for support to shelter arriving asylum seekers as the city faces an immediate need for additional capacity. Our initial request is for shelter to accommodate 500 asylum seekers, but, as New York City continues to see numbers balloon, this estimate will increase as well.[32]

The hypocrisy was incredible. Here was a sanctuary city leader, now responsible for fifteen thousand illegal aliens in a city of 8.5 million residents, and he cries for help for less than 0.001 percent of the city's total population. In March of 2023, New York City is now providing housing for the thousands of illegal aliens in over one hundred and eighty hotels in the city with three- and four-star ratings. These illegal aliens receive three meals a day through room service, phones, clothing, incidentals, and cable television costing the taxpayers of New York over $5 million a day. How in any rational world is it okay to house people that broke your laws in beautiful hotels when your own struggling homeless population is turned out on the street because of overcrowding in subpar homeless shelters? Also, why is it okay for cities like Uvalde, El Paso, San Diego, El Centro, and Yuma to have to deal with millions of illegal aliens, but New York City cannot handle fifteen thousand and demands billions of dollars from the federal government? In comparison, the first month of January of 2023, the city of El Paso was flooded with over sixteen thousand illegal aliens that were arrested and released by the Border Patrol onto El Paso's city streets in two days, not counting the thousands that got away!

Washington, DC's Mayor Bowser had it a little worse than her colleague, Mayor Adams. DC is another proud sanctuary city, but when twenty thousand illegal aliens arrived on buses from the southern border, she declared this invasion of twenty thousand illegal aliens in the DC population of 5.4 million a "state of emergency." The nation's capital is where the elites walk around collecting power and money. It is a place of influence and beauty, not a place for the unwashed masses from countries around the globe. The illegal alien's place is with the American masses of unwashed. Bowser famously stated, "We're not a border town. We don't have an infrastructure to handle this type of and level of immigration to our city." She continued by exclaiming, "…we're not Texas."[33]

This statement perfectly captures the ignorant mindset of a liberal politician. First, "we're not a border town"—where does she think ten million plus illegal aliens are going to go once Biden releases them? Does Bowser honestly believe that these millions of uneducated and government-dependent people are just going to stop in these border towns and pitch a tent? And if she believes that, how do medium-sized cities like El Paso and small towns like Uvalde sustain themselves? Is El Paso, with a population of over six hundred thousand, supposed to grow overnight to a city the size of New York or DC?

The second part of this statement also lets you inside the warped thinking of a liberal politician, "We don't have an infrastructure to handle this…." You claim to be a sanctuary city, but the people in charge of DC have never prepared to have their offer accepted. If they claim to offer help, while never having the ability or intention of fulfilling their promise, they are sitting higher up on the moral ladder than the unwashed masses of America. Lastly, "we're not Texas." Because Texas is on the border and DC is over two thousand miles away, Texan Americans are on their own, even though the politicians from far away invite illegal aliens into our collective home. Texas governor Abbott clearly stated the obvious in a letter to President Biden, when the president did a photo op in Texas, far away from the border.

> Under President Trump, the federal government achieved historically low levels of illegal immigration. Under your watch, by contrast, America is suffering the worst illegal immigration in the history of our country. Your open-border policies have emboldened the cartels, who grow wealthy by trafficking deadly fentanyl and even human beings. Texans are paying an especially high price for your failure, sometimes with their very lives, as local leaders from your own party will tell you if given the chance.[34]

The pain and suffering are okay for Texas and not for DC, because, as Bowser stated, "we're not a border town."

The crème de la crème of hypocrisy occurred in the third location, the vacation homes of the rich and famous in Martha's Vineyard. Florida's Governor DeSantis bused fifty illegal alien Venezuelans right into the heart of Martha's Vineyard, and the locals lost it. These Venezuelans landed there during the off-season for tourism, so there were many available houses and hotels for the unwashed to live in. "Where are these people supposed to live? How are they going to work? Where will their kids go to school? Dear God, these people of color can't live next to us, go to our schools, movie theaters, or restaurants!" The residents of this paradise are millionaires and billionaires, and said "No, thank you, we don't want any of the colored unwashed in our lily-white world!" And so, these illegal aliens were quickly loaded back into buses and shipped to a nearby military base, and this little town went back to 100 percent all white, sans the Obama family, and all was okay.

A local Democratic State Representative, Dylan Fernandez, stated, "These people need immigration services, immigration attorneys, and resources…. We got no heads up. Governor Abbot and Ron DeSantis wanted to create as much chaos as possible."[35] My first question to another hypocritical liberal politician is, why is chaos times thousands okay in Texas and Florida? Why must the communities of those states shoulder the burden of millions of illegal aliens, when Martha's Vineyard cannot seem to manage fifty illegal aliens? The reasoning is always this: the Democrats have their heart in the right place, but this type of people and the situations they cause are for other towns to accommodate.

The time will come soon when there are no more hiding places for the millions of unwashed illegal aliens. That is when you will see the importance of walls, as they will be constructed overnight around the lands occupied by the elite. Reports are now coming out that groups of illegal aliens are migrating into every state in the country. Once these initial groups find a community, their families and countrymen will flock to those locations. Small towns, cities, and states will be changed forever. Schools will be inundated with multiple language requests that cannot be filled. A case in point: I recently received a text from a Border Patrol source in San Diego that they are no longer just arresting Mexicans. The vast majority of the illegal aliens are now OTM (Other Than Mexican). My source just listed the countries from their daily arrests: Afghanistan, Cameroon, Eritrea, Kyrgyzstan, and Vietnam.

Now, imagine a family of Eritreans who are illegally paroled into the US and travel to and settle in, let's say, the town of Pella, Iowa, with a population of ten thousand. The demographic breakdown of Pella is 92 percent White, 3.5 percent Hispanic, and 2 percent Asian. I assume no one in the school district of Pella speaks Tigrinya. If not, they had better learn really quick! Let's imagine these families hit it off really well with their follow travelers from Kyrgyzstan, and they communicate by drawing pictures on loose pieces of paper they find along the trail from El Salvador. They use pictures because their friends from Kyrgyzstan speak both Russian and Kyrgyz. Amazingly, after giving up to the Border Patrol and being released, they are able to exchange cell numbers from their newly-issued government iPhones. The Eritreans invite the Kyrgyzstanis to visit this beautiful new land called Pella. The Kyrgyzstanis visit and have a wonderful time, so they decide to stay and grow roots in this community. I assure you that this scenario is happening everyday across America.

Here is another part of the Pella story that everyone wants to ignore, because of the fear of being called racist. The real truth about Americans is that we do not care about color. In spite of what the media and politicians claim, Americans love Americans and welcome Americans from other cities and states. We are not talking about Americans of different colors or ethnicities moving into Pella. What Americans do *not* want is serious demographic changes caused by artificial increases of people from other nations who do not speak English, share our societal norms, or understand our culture. America's birth rate is 1.64 per woman and declining. Eritrea's is 3.93 per woman and growing, and Kyrgyzstan's is at 3.00 per woman and also rising. This is not a racist statement—just data. Did anyone in Pella vote for a demographic change to their community?

Again, America and her opportunities are for America's citizens. If and when we decide to share these opportunities with foreign citizens, we will decide who and how many may come. This decision-making process is in the Constitution of the United States of America, and it gives only Congress the right to determine naturalization. The Supreme Court solidified this law found in Article 1, Section 8, Clause 4 and in Amendment XIV, Section 1. A president cannot just give an Executive Order and become king over immigration and naturalization. That can only be done by the Congress.

Biden has set new limits on parole to thirty thousand people a month from certain countries.[36] The border is in complete chaos, and Biden's remedy is to bring in thirty thousand more people through fraudulent means. After a calendar year, where are those three hundred and sixty thousand people going to reside? Pella?

The residents of Pella, Iowa, that are American citizens have protections by law from this invasion of their community, but nothing and no one will rescue them. They will just have to pound sand and hire as many English as a Second Language teachers as they can find. Within one generation, Pella will become unrecognizable, but Republicans will have more cheap labor and the Democrats will gain future voters.

What could happen in Pella is happening throughout America. We see it in big cities like Nashville, New York City, Washington, DC, and Minneapolis. We see it in small towns and cities and in states like Oregon, Illinois, Alabama, and North Carolina. The big cities and metropolitan areas are becoming saturated, causing all social services to rip apart at the seams. As these big cities become completely filled, these illegal immigrants will flow into smaller towns, causing demographic destruction. Because of the hundreds of different languages and cultures, even small towns will become balkanized. These communities will pit themselves against each other, and all these new arrivals will need every major kind of government assistance. The funding is finite, and thus, it will become scarce. Violence and crime will rise. Scarcity of goods, services, and jobs will cause frustration and anger. School resources will be funneled away from American children and into programs for the illegal alien children and their families. There will be demographic shifts causing residents to flee once prosperous neighborhoods. Outside of a new mom and pop restaurant serving an exotic menu, name one other positive aspect that this situation and thousands like it will produce. A time will come when infighting among the politicians and elites will begin, when the elites and politicians' lives are negatively affected by this mass invasion of illegal aliens. Not surprisingly, the first circular shots were just fired. Colorado Democratic Governor Jared Polis's life in late 2022 was interrupted by the endless waves of illegal aliens coming into his beautiful state. Colorado, in particular Denver, prides itself on being a sanctuary. Yet Governor Polis is doing the unthinkable and shipping the illegal aliens in his state to New York and Chicago.[37] The same Democrats and the liberal media howled about racism and xenophobia and claimed DeSantis and Abbot used migrants as pawns but said nothing about their liberal brother. The Denver Mayor Michael Hancock—of course a liberal Democrat—did not wait for even a thousand illegal aliens to set up residence in his city, to pull the ripcord of the "state of emergency." All it took was 650 illegal aliens to make this mayor cry uncle as these illegal aliens, "put an immense strain on city resources to the level where they're on the verge of reaching a breaking point at this time."[38] The hypocrisy from Colorado, DC, Martha's Vineyard, and New York City tells the true intentions of sanctuary cities and states. They simply are all talk and no action.

Mayor Adams of New York City made this laughable claim as a sanctuary city, "We're pointing the finger…at our national government. This is a national problem."[39] Really Mayor? Prior to your city being used as a trash can for the unwashed, you made demonstrative statements of support for Biden and your sanctuary city status. What changed? Now you are saying, "hold up, we can't handle anymore."

Polis answered Adams's and other criticisms by stating, "There is a lot of pent-up demand right now and a lot of frustration among our migrants who have been trapped for a week or two in a place they didn't want to be through no fault of their own."[40] Wait—what? These illegal aliens are frustrated because they crossed into our country against our laws, took our money and free iPhones, and then traveled across our nation at the expense of American taxpayers to places that they did not like and wanted to go elsewhere. How unfair of us.

This imbecile of a governor states that these same illegal aliens are not culpable at all for their situation, and now the

Governor's solution is to ship hundreds and thousands of his illegal aliens to other states like New York and Illinois. Are you telling me that Chicago needs further issues in that war zone of a city? I cannot wait until the Mexican Mafia, MS13, the Russian Mafia, and other violent gangs descend into the fray in Chicago. What could possibly go wrong?

The manifestation of corruption and criminal defiance of the Constitution will drive this nation into chaos. It will continue to balkanize our nation causing fractures within communities and states.

CHAPTER 8
How?

THE *HOW* PART of this equation to destroy the immigration system is unknown and ignored, because the deception is done within the policies and procedures of the Border Patrol, ICE, and the parent agency DHS. Nothing on this grand scale of malicious intent is by happenstance—it is thought out and then executed. As in any successful plan, you must correct course and make changes as outside forces push and pull. Since 1965, the politicians and elites have a true north, and they are dead set on getting there. They adjust course when they push too hard for amnesty or when they create coalitions that get discovered. Republicans Lyndsey Graham and the late John McCain, in collusion with Democrats, have betrayed the American citizens on the issue of immigration. Both men never met an immigration bill they did not love and push. In the battle of immigration control, Graham and McCain are both frauds.

However, the Biden administration is different from past administrations—it is aggressive and emboldened. The Biden administration feels a deep sense of urgency, as if this is their chance to create a historic change in America and right all her wrongs.

Past administrations have tried to aggressively push this decades-long destructive immigration plan, some succeeding with big wins, like the Reagan Amnesty and the Obama prosecutorial discretion. Others have failed like the Gang of Eight headed by Graham and McCain. Presidents Clinton and Bush tried to soft pedal and play both sides, but ultimately, they showed their true colors and favored foreign nationals over their constituents. Biden and his minions have studied the past presidents and feel both a sense of urgency and opportunity.

The Biden administration has taken Obama's platform of prosecutorial discretion and criminal neglect, and accelerated the number of border crossers to historic numbers. Any rational nation would have already placed their military on the border, but that would be countries that did not want this problem. We are now over nine thousand arrests every day. That number is on a trajectory that will reach ten thousand arrests daily within months, if not weeks. The number of getaways will increase exponentially to the arrests. We can expect daily crossings to surpass twenty thousand.

When the Democrats are successful in their treachery, no matter in what sector of government the disloyalty is occurring, they become so arrogant that they actually tell the world what they are doing. This occurred in January 2023, when Biden was in Mexico City with Mexican President Andres Manuel Lopez Obrador, and Canadian Prime Minister Justin Trudeau. Biden stated flatly, "We're trying to make it easier for people to get here—opening up the capacity to get here."[41] This is a direct quote from a press conference talking about immigration between the two countries. Biden is so arrogant and he knows that no one and nothing is going to stop him.

President Obrador confirms Biden's infidelity to his oath in one sentence, "You, President Biden, you are the first president of the United States in a very long time that has not built, not even one meter of wall, and that we thank you for that, sir."[42] The president of the nation that has for decades abused and trampled on our nation's sovereignty, and has facilitated the rest of the world to travel through his country to also trample on our sovereignty, is thanking our leader for not stopping this invasion.

The mass invasion started with the organized caravans of hundreds of thousands of illegal aliens making the trek to the border, and then crossing as one mass of humanity to overwhelm the system. President Trump used all his powers to hold them back, but the day Biden was installed as president things changed quickly. As those hordes of humanity began to cross the border, the Border Patrol was quickly overwhelmed and then gave up, as we did not have any plan in place to handle the thousands that crossed.

I remember the franticness of those early days. When thousands of people were marching to the border wearing "We Love Biden" T-shirts, confirmation of a welcomed invasion was right in front of us. We all knew this situation was going to get worse. Endless buses were literally driving into our facility to unload hundreds of illegal aliens to be processed and housed, while other buses were leaving our facility to release hundreds of illegal aliens right into the communities where we lived. This cycle continued over and over, every day. Immediately, every Border Patrol facility was at daily maximum holding capacity, trying everything possible to not release them, to being forced to release hundreds to Non-Governmental Organizations (NGOs). Our government uses NGOs to both shield the government from culpability of transporting illegal aliens to their destination, and the NGOs help place illegal aliens throughout the nation as the US government does not have the infrastructure in place to handle millions of human smuggling transactions. Immediately after partnering with NGOs to "wash our hands," the NGOs were overwhelmed. The Border Patrol was essentially drowning in illegal aliens with nowhere to put them, so we just released them, many times right out the front door of our station.

I remember standing outside of our offices in the Murrieta Border Patrol Station with my Patrol Agent in Charge (PAIC) and watching the criminality of the situation play out in front of us. We would stand outside in stunned disbelief as our life's work was being destroyed in front of us. Every Border Patrol Agent was demoralized.

The buses never stopped even while COVID was rampaging through the country. The NGOs would test the illegal aliens for COVID, then split them into two buses—one COVID-positive and one COVID-negative. The positive bus would go to hotels in a popular tourist location in San Diego, and the negative bus went straight to a bus station where they were released. These hotels, along with three meals a day and unlimited medical attention, were paid for by the federal government, for fourteen nights of quarantine, if they wanted. Another part of this insanity was that these COVID-positive individuals were allowed to leave if they wanted. There was no law enforcement to hold them at these hotels for medical isolation. We received many reports that these illegal aliens with COVID would just leave the hotel and disappear.

While American citizens were locked down in our homes and told that we had to stay at home and limit all movement with many strict guidelines, millions of illegal aliens were given a complete pass to ignore all US policies and guidelines around COVID protocols and to travel freely, all while being COVID-positive. It was insanity at a scale I never thought would happen in my career. We have hundreds of thousands of homeless people in our country—many veterans without a dry and warm place to sleep—because we have turned over numerous shelters to illegal aliens. Do you see a despicable pattern of "America last?" When did taking care of other nation's citizens become more important and more compassionate than caring for our own brothers and sisters of America?

The process of arresting, transporting, and processing millions of illegal aliens a year caused the system to collapse. All ICE and Border Patrol facilities were busting at the seams, creating makeshift holding facilities, tents, and "cages." In Texas, they constructed holding facilities for five hundred to a thousand people, but up to twenty-five hundred individuals would be held in a tent three-fourths the size of a football field, as the illegal aliens moved through some part of the processing assembly line.

The politicians knew from past presidential immigration debacles that they needed to quickly change policies within the DHS, so it could stay ahead of the information the citizens of our country received outside the mainstream media. DHS had to make changes to some part of the pipeline from arrest to release. The government also knew that the American people would not tolerate simple street releases that were just NTAs but would have to bamboozle the American people with a new category of casework used by the Border Patrol and ICE. The government's answer was to pencil-whip casework into a single page or two and quickly process thousands a day to allow these illegal aliens to fraudulently claim asylum, because it was quicker and more efficient to push these people out into our streets. The government then claimed the moral high ground stating that its hands were tied, and it had to process and release these asylum cases. This was all a lie.

The government relied on the ignorance of the American people—that the media would never factually report the truth about asylum. Asylum seekers, per intentional law, must apply to the first safe country from the country they are trying to escape. That meant that the millions of individuals trying to get to America to make a claim for asylum had to first apply in the first safe country that they entered. Mexico would be that country for most of these people. That was the "Remain in Mexico" policy—also called "Migrant Protection Protocols"— that Trump enforced, and Biden abolished as quickly as he could. Also, asylum law states that individuals who apply for asylum must present themselves at a Port of Entry or an America Embassy, and that individual must wait outside of the US. Incredibly, the Biden administration wanted all asylum petitioners to be allowed to wait in the US. President Biden's administration forced DHS, and in turn the Border Patrol, to ignore this requirement. This meant the millions of border-crossers would not have to present themselves at a Port of Entry; instead, they could jump the border and squat. Border Patrol Agents would eventually pick them up, transport them to the station, and quickly process and release them as asylum seekers. The whole asylum situation is just theater.

Out of the hundreds of Republican lawmakers, only several have the courage to speak the truth, and one stands out as a voice of reason and a voice of contempt for the traitors inside our government.[43] His name is Representative Chip Roy of Texas. In 2023, he submitted a bill titled H.R. 29,[44] which would grant the Secretary of DHS the ability to deny all asylum claims and reject current asylum claimants in the US, using detention capacity thresholds as a measure to trigger the bill's enforcement rules. This bill would allow state Attorney Generals to sue the federal government if these measures were not enforced. Congressman Roy knows Mayorkas and the Biden administration will never enforce any law that slows or impedes the flow of millions of illegal aliens into our nation. Of course, the moment Congressman Roy placed this bill on the congressional calendar, over 250 human rights and refugee groups condemned it. If these anti-American groups denounce a bill that is going to stop the immigration debacle, then the bill must be passed! Let's look at a quote from Aaron Reichlin-Melnick, Policy Director of the American Immigration Council:

"Not only does this bill *require* the end to asylum until literally every single person crossing can be detained (which is currently physically impossible), it also gives DHS a permanent discretionary authority to end asylum at every border" (emphasis from Reichlin-Melnick).

What Mr. Reichlin-Melnick admits is, because of the lack of will from DHS, he believes that there is no way to stop the illegal entry of millions of people coming into America. This lack of will comes from the current discretionary authority of the DHS being abused by Mayorkas—the same discretionary authority Mr. Reichlin-Melnick is okay with when it is for lawlessness, but believes it is bad when that authority is used to protect America. Opposition to this bill is not only from the far left and their activist partners but from Republicans like Congressman Tony Gonzales from Texas who believes that open borders and completely closed borders are both bad ideas. The battle for the sovereignty of America will be fought against both political parties, for the treason and anti-America beliefs held by the Democrats and Republicans are deeply rooted.

There are less than one thousand Asylum Officers in the DHS, which now claims that the wait time for an asylum seeker to see an Immigration Judge is over six years! By just doing simple math, I know that timeline is a lie. Asylum Officers have been overwhelmed and are pushing out approved asylum claims at a rate of over 90 percent. It must be noted that a large portion of Asylum Officers are former immigration defense lawyers. To help these officers, Border Patrol Agents were cross-trained as Asylum Officers. I know several of these Agents. An extremely intelligent Supervisory Border Patrol Agent described the scene in the asylum world as a world completely engulfed in fraud. He stated that every individual's story, depending on their country of origin, was the same. Each country had its own prepared statement. Many times, the only part of the story that was different was the name of the street the individual used. My former colleague stated that there was no way any of these asylum claims should have been approved.

The Border Patrol Agents took control of this system and turned it upside down. The 90 percent approval rate flipped to 90 percent declination, but the DHS did not want to hear anything from Asylum Officers except "approved." So, after several months of incredible success, the Border Patrol unit of cross-trained Asylum Officers were disbanded. Highly productive and intelligent Border Patrol Agents were told to just go away. If you forced these Asylum Officers to work every day, including weekends, with no time off, and expected them to complete nine cases a day (an impossible task), they would only be able to handle the daily illegal entries and asylum claims.

The system is broken, and it is intentional. Think about the overall treasonous plan from the traitor's point of view: they know in another two years of Biden being in charge with no Republican effort to block him, there will be another twenty million illegal aliens who will enter into our country with at least five to seven million of them being processed for asylum. Those one thousand Asylum Officers will never, in one hundred careers, be able to make a dent in the number of asylum cases.

In January 2023, the game changed again. The asylum system is so completely unworkable that the DHS had to add another avenue to help accelerate the flow of people: Immigration Parole. NTAs take an Agent some time to complete, and asylum cases a little less, but still too much time, as the number of border crossers increases daily. To the credit of the DHS led by Secretary Mayorkas, they know when to pivot and make necessary course corrections.

Agents are now told to process the majority of illegal aliens as a "Parole case." Now, let me explain that difference between the term "Parole" in state and local law enforcement, compared to federal immigration law enforcement. "State Parole" is an agreement between the state and the inmate that the inmate receives early release from prison, with terms attached, including scheduled check-in dates, drug tests, and a promise to not commit further crimes. If these and other terms are not met, the inmate goes back to prison. "Immigration Parole" is completely different. Federal immigration law enforcement uses

Immigration Parole to bring in foreign nationals as material witnesses to a crime or for several humanitarian reasons. This parole is set for a relatively short amount of time. Let's say an ICE Officer paroles a Mexican citizen into the US to testify as a witness to a human smuggling event. That Mexican national would be paroled for ten days. After those ten days and prior to that Mexican citizen returning to Mexico, he would check in with an immigration official to declare his return to his home country. Immigration Parole was rarely used, tightly supervised, and controlled. Not now.

The DHS has taken this lawful policy and procedure and corrupted it. What the DHS is forcing Border Patrol Agents to do is illegal, but the DHS does not care—who will do anything about it? Take that same Haitian family we discussed in an earlier chapter. In this parole scenario, that family is not given an NTA. They are still told to report to an ICE facility near its imaginary Nashville residence. This family is put into the DHS database to check any prior deportations and/or criminal arrests (which is irrelevant because they are all released), then processed for Immigration Parole. This entire process takes minimal time and then that family is released into the US. The Immigration Parole states that this Haitian family has sixty days to report to an ICE facility, where it will be given an NTA. To an immigration official this sounds insane and completely implausible. To the public it sounds not perfect, but acceptable.

In real life, this family never makes it to Nashville because they do not even know if Nashville is a city or another planet in our solar system. Nashville is just part of the script written for them by their smuggler. When the sixty-day window expires, this entire family is considered illegal aliens. My ICE sources state that over 90 percent of these Parole cases never present themselves to an ICE facility, and they abscond into the wind.

What is so masterful about this DHS plan is that there is not one federal agency that will locate and then deport these illegal Haitians. This family of four will live and work illegally in our country waiting for the magical amnesty to appear. This family is the Democrat's future voters, being forced to work for low wages so the Chamber of Commerce and corporations throughout our economy can make more money, then funnel a small portion of that to politicians for their re-election campaigns. Everyone wins, except for the American citizen.

The latest lawlessness is the CBP One App.[45] Yes, the Biden administration thinks that you are so dumb and distracted that it has created an app for people still in foreign countries who want to apply for asylum. Biden is so empowered that he actually created a way to reach down into the southern nations and pull them into our country under fraudulent asylum claims.

We have a backlog of millions of illegal asylum claimants, but instead of implementing what Congressman Roy wants to do with H.R. 29, our government tries with all its collective might to make it easier for people to come into our country. DHS officials are calling this "smart border innovation."

There will be absolutely zero security controls. The DHS claims facial recognition will play a major role, but what about the millions of asylum claimants that have absconded, never to be seen again? What good will facial recognition do?

Mayorkas claims, "We are working tirelessly to rebuild our immigration system."[46] Stop for a second and reread that sentence. He is "trying to rebuild the immigration system." Remember, as I have written previously that they claim the system is broken, but no one understands how it broke or who broke it, and only they can fix it. It's like being a teenager and you come home in your dad's car with the passenger side caved in. Your dad is pissed and you lie to him claiming, "Someone must have smashed into your car when I was in the movies. But don't worry dad, I am investigating who smashed your car."

I look to my party, the Republicans, and I see an old man that looks like a turtle—Mitch McConnell—who is completely in bed with the Democrats. He has been in office longer than I have been alive and has done nothing but hurt America on the issue of the border and illegal immigration. I look to the House for help, and I see only a handful of leaders with the courage or the intellect to challenge the brazen America-last haters as they drive us straight into total destruction. There is not much hope.

The internal manipulation of laws and policies do the most damage—it is the greatest part of the *how*. The final step in the *how* is the Democrats creating a false narrative. When the Democrats, masters of projection, blame the Republicans, you can be sure the Democrats are doing the same thing in spades. From the White House, Biden blamed the Republicans for the open border invasion. He stated with absolute certainty, "Cracking down on illegal immigration, strengthening legal immigration, and protecting dreamers, those with temporary protective status, like farm workers, are part of the fabric of our nation. But congressional Republicans have refused to consider my plan and they rejected my retest for an additional $3.5 billion to secure the border and funds the 2,000 new asylum personnel."[47]

Where do I even begin with this monster lie? First, when did you start cracking down on illegal aliens? I just wrote about the Mexican president praising Biden for not building one meter of the wall. Old Joe wants two thousand additional asylum officers. Why? Because the thousand asylum officers you have now are drowning in paperwork and cannot rubber-stamp the fraudulent asylum cases fast enough. In this same press statement this bumbling idiot says, "20,000 pounds of fentanyl is enough to kill as many as 1,000 people in this country."[48] First, that much fentanyl, which is only a small fraction of what is safely smuggled across our open borders, could kill four and a half billion people!

Our government has normalized this insanity—this is the *how*.

America has come to expect treasonous action against the body of America. We have been beaten into a submissive citizenry. We have allowed our freedom to be slowly and intentionally taken from us without a single shot being fired. We have allowed the enemy within to steal our country from us. Our founding fathers, the best generation, and all the men and women that have died for this nation are ashamed of us. I fear we are becoming that generation that Reagan spoke about, "Freedom is never more than one generation away...."[49]

CHAPTER 9
The Other Borders

People rightfully focus on the southern border, but the coastal borders are also wide open. Maritime narcotics and human smuggling have gone unchecked—there is basically zero maritime law enforcement on either coast.

Florida and California are ground zero for this maritime smuggling. Florida had to close the Dry Tortugas National Park because of migrant boats washing ashore—for example, over three hundred Cubans—causing havoc and panic. This is happening daily in Florida. On Fox and Friends, Rick Ramsey, Florida sheriff from Monroe County, stated that the illegal alien surge is destroying his department's resources to protect his residents. He sums up the frustration and resentment of local law enforcement toward Biden and his administration's response to this illegal alien surge:

> ...very manpower intensive. I'm having to pull resources all day long to respond to landings where we're diverting police, fire, rescue, and we're dealing with just a mass migration for us, for a rural county, we consider a mass

migration. And we are worried about the humanitarian crisis about this going on. Border Patrol is overwhelmed at our level that we're having groups of migrants having to sit on the side of the road for long periods of time waiting to be picked up, processed, or taken care of. We actually had the other day, we called for a pickup for a group of migrants, they were so busy they told us they may not be able to arrive until the following day. So, we're like, what are we supposed to do, leave a group of women and children and kids on the side of the road for a day, day and a half? No bathrooms, no food, no shelter. So, it's a little concerning. I'm overall worried about the public safety of my citizens in Monroe. This does affect my ability to do my job to protect, serve, patrol, and take care of my citizens.

He added,

We just want the government to have an actual working plan that works for this geographic area. Every area's different. But this is nothing that wasn't foreseeable. We've spoken to the government in the past, we said, this is increasing. This is going to be a problem; you need to work on an action plan now so we can mitigate this when it does occur. Now, it's occurring to what we thought, and there's not much of a plan.[50]

The lawlessness of the immigration disaster is now targeting the coastlines. On New Year's Day 2023, Chief Patrol Agent Walter Slosar of Miami Sector tweeted out a picture of two abandoned fishing vessels, stating, "Over 160 migrants have been encountered today in the Florida Keys. Border Patrol agents with support from federal, state, and local LE partners responded to 10 migrant landings since midnight."[51] Ten landings in one day! Every law enforcement entity having to partake in immigration is now stretched to the max, with no capacity to help more.

There is a reoccurring theme throughout this intentional immigration debacle: Biden and his turncoats willfully ignore all pleas from law enforcement agencies and departments to do something—anything. Then, they force these same local law enforcement departments to exacerbate their finite funds. Just like on the land borders, coastal law enforcement only knows what actually lands on the coast when they sit there and give up. As my friend and Border Patrol Supervisor asked me the other day, "J. J., everyone we arrest gets released. So why do you think people are running through the open border where there are no Agents patrolling instead of just crossing the border and squatting?" I didn't need to answer him because we both knew exactly why. Imagine the numbers and types of people that are landing and absconding: criminals, terrorists, and previously deported felons who know that if caught they are going to jail or are going to be deported.

The West Coast is even more active than the East Coast. The human and narcotic smuggling routes through the Pacific Ocean are lucrative since there is not one maritime unit working the coastline. I intimately know this coast, and the law enforcement strategy that works here, because I created and supervised a maritime unit that fought the narcotic and human smugglers.

This unit was called the Coastal Border Enforcement Team, or CBET for short. Our AOR was from La Jolla, CA, to Santa Barbara, CA, which is over 175 coastal miles. In my unit, I had forty Border Patrol Agents from two Border Patrol stations, ten Los Angeles/Long Beach Office of Field Operations Officers (OFO), and a dozen California National Guardsmen. I take great pride in the creation and growth of this unit, because we were the first of its kind in law enforcement, which is rare. There are maritime boat units on both coasts as well as the United States Coast Guard, but never before was there a law enforcement unit that worked the coastline and intercepted the maritime loads as they landed on the beaches.

I remember being given the assignment of creating CBET. I was assigned four Border Patrol Agents, three vehicles, and an old Vietnam-era infrared camera that was useless. One of my Agents was a Trainee, and the other three had not passed their two years mark (not the best team—yet). The border in San Diego Sector was one of the few sectors across the southern border that was working back in 2009, because of the amount of money and Agents that were poured into San Diego. The Tijuana–San Diego border was difficult to cross, so the path of least resistance was the Pacific Ocean. The smugglers' maritime vessel of choice was the open-bow fishing vessel called a *panga*. The pangas were thirty-five to fifty feet long and twenty feet wide with a depth of ten feet. At first, pangas with one engine were washing ashore almost every other night. Many times, witness reports stated up to thirty-five people would run across the beach from the beached panga and into waiting vans and box trucks. I was stationed at the San Clemente Border Patrol Station which sat alongside I-5 and Camp Pendleton Marine Corps Base, forty-five miles north of the international border.

My unit's AOR started down south in La Jolla, CA. La Jolla means "The Jewel," and the town is just that—a jewel. The coastline is spectacular, with multimillion dollar homes lining the high cliffs above the Pacific Ocean. The first few months CBET was chasing our tails. We didn't have the manpower, technology, or experience. Each night was one failure after another, and I was pissed. I am not the type of guy to take failure lightly, so I immediately went on a mission to acquire more men and equipment. I also took a good hard look at the landscape of maritime smuggling and made bold decisions. I cobbled together ten Agents from San Clemente Border Patrol Station and another ten Agents from Murrieta Border Patrol Station. I partnered with a Supervisor from Los Angeles/Long Beach OFO, and they gave me ten men. I also received cutting edge technology; CBET was assigned two high-powered infrared cameras called Forward Looking InfraRed, or FLIR for short. These cameras were game changers because they could break through up to seven miles of the intense darkness of the ocean night. I had thirty young, excitable, and ambitious Agents, two cameras, and several decent unmarked vehicles. What could go wrong?

Our learning curve was steep, but we climbed over it and began the journey of becoming experts in this new law enforcement area. We quickly learned the tactics of the smugglers. For the first two years, the human smugglers owned these routes; we were arresting panga-loads of over thirty people per maritime event.

Then overnight, everything changed. One night at Calafia State Beach in San Clemente, California—which is famous for President Nixon's home on the coast—I responded to one of my Agents who spotted a panga just off the shoreline. We were so stretched out geographically that I was the only Agent in the area. I snuck down into the parking lot of Calafia State Beach. It was two o'clock in the morning with no moonlight at all. Trying to conceal myself, I walked along a rocky base of small hills that shaped the coastline. I could not see any panga beached on the shoreline, but I continued to walk along the base of the hill. After about fifty feet, I walked up on six young men, all wearing black clothes. My first thought was that the panga had landed, dropped off only six people, and gone back out in the ocean. I immediately used my broken Spanish to tell them all to get on the ground. They just looked at me, until one of these young men said, "Why you speaking Spanish?" Stunned, I stopped for a second trying to understand what was happening. My radio communications with my FLIR Operator did not work, as usual along the beaches. I told the six men to kneel on the beach. The same guy that asked me why I was speaking Spanish motioned for the other five to circle around me as he said, "We don't have to fucking listen to you!" I did not know what was happening, but I knew it was associated with the panga, and having six men circle around was not good. I did exactly what I had done for a decade on the border: I reacted quickly with maximum force. I clubbed the leader, who went flying into the air and slammed onto the rocks, and—just as usual on the border—the others were cowards who wanted nothing to do with me or the violence they had just witnessed.

I had all six men prone out on the sandy beach until backup arrived. I finally got communication with my FLIR Operator, who told me the panga had never landed and that there were only two people on board. The FLIR sees heat signatures that can clearly make out the pangas and everything inside them, like humans and packages. This panga had only two people and a lot of packages.

It all made sense now. These six men were mules for a narcotics load, and I had spooked the boat captain. We were able to track the panga, using our new FLIR, to a new beach community in Dana Point, CA (a community where Oprah had a house). Sure enough, we located two individuals hiding in the cliffs under this neighborhood of multimillion-dollar homes. Back at the panga were a couple of thousand pounds of narcotics. The entire maritime environment changed that night, because now we knew the narco cartels had learned that the human smugglers had found a successful route using the Pacific Ocean. Human smugglers are lowlife scum, but the power, violence and money is in the narco cartels, who then muscled their way into the Pacific Ocean.

Rarely, if ever, again did we encounter a human-smuggling load. The size of the pangas grew to the size of school buses. The number of high-powered engines loaded on these fishing vessels went from one to three or four, depending on the size of the narcotic load and the distance they would travel. The size of the narcotics in pounds went from one thousand pounds a load to six thousand to ten thousand pounds per load. The number of people needed to smuggle these loads increased to well over twenty. And the violence increased as the cost of the cargo rose and because of the type of person who worked for the cartels.

In the next few years, CBET arrested over 150 maritime events. We were a motley crew of dudes, but we became the experts in this field. As the maritime smugglers traveled further up the coast, I would have to take my unit further up the coast as well. There are small beach cities along the Pacific Ocean coastline with their own sheriffs or police departments. Every time I went into a new jurisdiction, I would have to meet the brass, and the meetings always went the same way. These local law enforcement departments were small and they assigned their best, usually a group of detectives, to work with CBET. We would meet with our new partners at a 10:00 p.m. muster at their station, usually sitting at the station's huge conference table with the plain clothes detectives and lieutenants in uniform. Many of my guys wore shorts and T-shirts, all had huge beards and long hair. We looked so bad that in every one of our first meetings with a new department, I would start the meeting by stating, "I know we look like a ragtag bunch of dudes, but we are the greatest at what we do." Despite the look of our unit, our reputation as tough and fearless Agents grew with each new arrest. Our AOR was so big, I would assign a small group of Agents a large coastal area each night. These small groups of Agents knew that the entire CBET Unit would have their back, but that it would take hours to get there. This built camaraderie and trust, because the Agents in that small group were all we had.

One night, I took five Agents to Santa Barbara, because we had intel that a large narcotic load was going to come ashore sometime in the early hours the following morning. All six of us began the three- to four-hour drive north, starting out at six o'clock in the evening, to get to Santa Barbara to set up and be ready for the maritime smuggling event. We got up to Santa Barbara, set up, and waited and waited until the sun came up, but no panga. Disappointed, we made an even longer drive back to the station, as we had to drive through Los Angeles morning rush hour. Midnights are rough on the body and mind, not to mention adding six hours of driving. On the drive, I spoke with the Intel Agent, and he told me that they had tracked the panga all the way to the southern edge of Santa Barbara and the panga returned to Mexican waters without landing.

I had told the other Agents in my small unit that we would come into work at the regular time at 10:00 p.m. I went home and immediately fell asleep. I woke up and thought about what the Intel Agent had told me, and it didn't make sense. By around seven o'clock that evening, I couldn't shake the feeling that the intel given to me was wrong—I had never experienced a panga making a two-hundred-mile journey all the way to their destination to not land and return to Mexico with their cargo. I called my right-hand man and told him to tell the other Agents to get to the station and gear up—we were going back to Santa Barbara.

We were behind the clock as we raced up to Refugio State Park in Santa Barbara. I called my partner that works for the California State Parks and asked for any help he could give me. He gave me two Rangers. Before we all got to Refugio, I had two of my five Agents from our unit set up a mile from the expected panga landing site with their FLIR. The rest of us got to Refugio at about 11:45 p.m., met the two State Park Rangers, and talked to the infrared scope operator that was assigned to CBET from the California National Guard. Within fifteen minutes, a large panga with three outboard engines appeared on the FLIR monitor about three miles offshore. There were three individuals on the panga and it was loaded with narcotic packages. My FLIR guys called me saying that a large RV just dropped off twenty-five individuals who were walking down to the beach from the highway. I told the three Agents with me to jump into the bed of my unmarked truck as we would have to drive the narrow beach trails south for about two miles without using the vehicle's lights. I turned to the two

Rangers and asked which one knew the trails best. The taller one confidently stated, "I do—I have been on the job longer." I asked, "Well, how long have you been a Ranger?" The tall Ranger answered proudly, "I just passed my first year on the job!" Stunned, I asked the other Ranger what his time on duty was, and he responded sheepishly, "I am still on training. I have been on for three months." Dear God, I am going headfirst into another huge narcotic-smuggling event with three other Agents with less than three years on the job and two nugget Rangers. I hadn't liked being in this type of scenario numerous times before and I didn't like it now, but it had become normal to me. Unnerving, but normal.

The "senior" Ranger jumped into the passenger seat and everyone else jumped into the bed of my Ford Raptor truck. We maneuvered up and down the narrow beach trail on the cliffs above the coastline, using only the moonlight. We parked about two hundred yards away from the trail leading down to the sandy beach below, that the twenty-five mules had used. I made one last phone call to the two FLIR operators for a final update and told them to get to our location as quickly as they could, before we all turned our cell phones off and went communication-dark. (Our service radios were useless that far north on the coast.)

We made our way down the long beachhead trail to its base: me, three young but experienced CBET Agents, and two very young and inexperienced Park Rangers. We had done this before—I would have loved to have twenty other CBET Agents with me, but this was enough. I was in the front of my team because you can't lead from any other position. The US Attorneys wanted one of us to visually see every mule touch a narcotic package, in order to strengthen their case. I never understood why they wanted this, but they were the bosses on that side of the law, so we followed their instructions. I was hiding behind a scraggy bush with my team lined up behind me. I watched each and every mule grab a ninety-pound narcotic package from the panga. Each bundle was wrapped tightly with thick black waterproof wrapping. Each mule walked the heavy bundles approximately seventy-five yards from the panga to the beach trail, right to my position, then dropped the package in a large pile. This went on for several minutes, as the panga floated quietly with its engines off in the low tide about thirty yards offshore. I turned to my team and our two new CBET Rangers and said softly, "On my go." I turned around just as one of the mules was dropping another package of narcotics into the pile. This time he stopped and looked right at the bush I was hiding behind, as he was trying to comprehend why there was someone on the other side of the bush. That's all I needed to see and it was go time!

Our rule was that the first Agent out would go straight for the panga, because once the boat captain turned those engines on, it would be out to sea within seconds, never to be found. As I led my ragtag team out to the beach, I announced "Border Patrol" as I ran by the mule staring at me. I ran another ten feet into the chaos of the mules running as far away from us as possible, I ran over a mule and then slammed another to the ground, as all I wanted to do was get on that panga before it left. My team was arresting the mules as fast as they could catch them and I was running as fast as I could to the shoreline. I could see the three boat captains scrambling to get the engines started. My pace slowed as I ran into the water. I tried as hard as I could to run with my knees as high as I could get them, so I could move faster through the water. When I got to the panga, I could hear the three men yelling at each other in Spanish. I jumped up and grabbed hold of the edge of the panga several feet above me, and pulled myself up and over into the panga, on top of large narcotic packages. I stood up on top of the jumbled packages as the panga gently rocked back and forth with the low tide. One of the boat captains jumped into the dark water trying to escape, another quickly abandoned the ship, and finally, it was only me and the last boat captain, who was standing behind the wheel of the vessel. I knew from experience that there would be a large screwdriver and a large knife or machete by the steering console, because every panga captain had them. I also knew that if this smuggler could get the engines started, we would be out to sea within seconds. Both those situations would be bad, and I knew I wasn't going to be stabbed, nor was I going out to sea to my death.

I was at the front of this huge panga about forty feet from the boat captain. I pulled out my service weapon, sighted the smuggler in, and told him in my best Spanish, "Don't turn the engine on or I will kill you." I stepped slowly over the large packages toward the smuggler, watching for him to make a move, as I told him, "*Esto es me launcha! Brincar! Ahora!*" ("This is my boat! Get off! Now!") He stared at me, looked out at the darkness and the freezing water, then back to me, shaking his head no. I was now standing about five feet away and about three feet above him on the large narcotic bundles. I holstered my weapon, went deep inside myself, and channeled my best impression of King Leonidas in *300* when he kicked the enemy's messenger into the city's deep well. I jumped down toward him, kicking him squarely in his chest, and yelled, "This is my panga!" The smuggler went flying into the moonlit night, splashing violently into the freezing water. I stood on my panga and watched my team of five CBET Agents and two California State Park Rangers arrest twenty-five mules and three boat captains. We seized the RV that had dropped off the mules, and we seized *my* panga. We seized El Chapo Guzman's Sinaloa Cartel's seven thousand pounds of narcotics.

Over several years, we shut the maritime smuggling down completely. By 2014, we had arrested just a few maritime events—the furthest north was north of Pescadero State Beach, south of San Francisco—and the Pacific Ocean was no longer the safest and easiest smuggling route for the cartels. In 2015, the war was over and we had won. One of my Agents testified against El Chapo in his criminal case and helped secure a conviction. Those one-hundred-plus men and women that worked for me and in our CBET Unit/Family are heroes. The politicians that betray us and our nation and slam us for fulfilling our oath can all go to hell.

My former colleagues now tell me that pangas are landing all over the place in San Diego and beyond. They cannot even guess what the true number of maritime incursions is because there are no more CBET Units. The Agents that worked on CBET during the Trump years are all processing and transporting illegal aliens. Just like on the land borders, the coastal borders are now completely open.

Let me tell you a story that is as relevant today as it was back in 2010 when I had a meeting with the Provost Marshall of Marine Corps Base Camp Pendleton. The Provost Marshall for the Marines is their law enforcement entity on base. I had a meeting with the Provost Marshall because panga captains were using the Landing Craft, Air Cushion (LCAC) tower's lights as a guide to land. The LCAC Tower is huge and stands several stories high, right on the shoreline of the Marine Corps

Base Camp Pendleton and is used for the navy hovercrafts. The LCAC hovercraft landing area has a huge concrete runway from the shoreline to the hovercraft hangers. This is an extremely sensitive and secure area and was completely off limits to anyone without special clearance.

What I write next is truly unbelievable, but here it goes. The smugglers would line up their panga ten miles offshore using the LCAC's powerful lights to guide them ashore. Once they landed, they would jump out of the panga and all thirty or more of these individuals would run straight up the same concrete runway as the hovercrafts use. This large group would then run across the west side of the Marine Corps base and climb over a security fence onto I-5 and into their vehicles waiting to take them north into America.

I honestly could not believe this was happening right on a navy installation on the famous and powerful Camp Pendleton Marine Corps Base. I met with the Provost Marshall and asked for access into the LCAC area and tower and any help the Marines could give me. I stressed the importance of securing this area and the importance of arresting everyone that comes off these pangas, because of national security. The Provost Marshall smirked when I said national security, and we all just stopped talking and looked at each other. I paused as I looked around the room, and then I looked right at the Provost and his men and said, "We have no idea who has come off these pangas. We have intelligence stating that there are terrorist cells in Mexico and once they learn that they can get direct access onto Camp Pendleton undetected, game over." The room got a little uneasy, but I continued, "I know it sounds improbable but I wonder what you would have said to me on September tenth if I said terrorists would highjack airplanes and fly them into the

World Trade Centers?" We got complete access to the LCAC Tower. My conversation with the Provost Marshall all the way back in 2010 is the same conversation America should be having every day. The coastal waterways and shorelines are wide open. The land borders in the south and north are completely unprotected. Because these borders are unprotected, America is vulnerable to attack. What nation in the history of civilization would allow this to happen? How real is this terrorist maritime threat? In April 2023, nineteen suspected terrorists associated with the Islamic State and Iranian cells made a maritime landing on the UK shoreline. Seven of the nineteen are under active investigations.[52] The world is very small, and I am sure the terrorists from the Middle East have shared the information that the United States is even more vulnerable than the UK. I would bet a month's salary that a terrorist cell has already made a successful maritime landing in the United States, or they are planning to make an attempt shortly.

One of the most poignant memes I have seen was a picture of a strong man, obviously a veteran, standing proud with a sign that said, "When the United States falls, there will be no one coming to help. We are it." That little meme strikes right at the heart of the issue. At this pace of millions of illegal aliens pouring into our country, we will self-destruct from within and there will be absolutely not one country that will come to our aid.

They will not come for several reasons. First, when that collapse happens there will be utter chaos and violence, frightening the world into self-preservation. Secondly, the world despises America, yet we are letting into our country the citizens of the world. At the minimum, the other countries across the globe would love for America to be brought down several levels. Lastly, the world will see a pot of gold to dig into instead of a country in need.

We are our own best hope. Americans need each other. We do not need the citizens of the world that have nothing in common with us, but only want to take what is ours. And do not be ashamed or embarrassed to say what we have is ours. Generations before us fought and died for this freedom and these opportunities. We are the men and women that continue to make America great. I am disgusted when these gutless politicians state we need these people because they work harder, have better family values, and are more entrepreneurial than Americans. That is beyond absurd. A reasonable person needs to ask just one question and these idiotic and incompetent politicians and elite's theory crumbles: "Why are the countries these people come from disasters economically, spiritually, and societally if they are all the things you claim?" We all know the answer. The fawning of illegal aliens by politicians shows their blatant animus of the people they represent.

Immigrants must accentuate what is already good in our country. Immigrants must enhance an already excellent way of life we live. Immigrants must be a net positive in all areas of life. If these immigrants cannot begin their lives here by first legally coming into our country, then all bets are off.

CHAPTER 10
"How?" Part II: ICE

WHAT IS HAPPENING on the backend of the *how* is equally important to what is happening on the front lines with the Border Patrol. The backend players in this treasonous is ICE. ICE plays an enormous role in locating, arresting, and then deporting illegal aliens from our country. The ICE units that focus on prior deported felons and violent criminals (including those released from sanctuary cities and states) have a profound mission. The height of irony is that the Left claim to care about minorities and their safety. Statistically proven, the previously deported criminal aliens terrorize these very same minority communities though gangs, drug dealing, violent sex assaults, and numerous other forms of criminality. The poor communities that these Democrats claim to care about are left defenseless and vulnerable to the same heinous criminals that Democrats protect.

ICE Officers are forced to follow the same unlawful orders and do the same illegal and immoral actions as Border Patrol Agents, just on the backside of this circus instead of the front lines. ICE Officers are equally demoralized and frustrated.

They can no longer do any enforcement activities. They are completely overwhelmed. Interior arrests by ICE Officers during the most recent "normal/non-pandemic numbers" of 2019 numbered approximately 267,000. In 2021, there were approximately 62,000. That is an almost 80 percent drop![53] That means hundreds of thousands of criminal illegal aliens are not deported from our country and continue to rape, murder, and pillage our countrymen. (I will write in detail in a later chapter how there is a standing army of illegal alien criminals in our nation that number in the millions.)

We have our own sociopaths and heinous criminals. When a mother or wife is raped, it is devastating. The murder of a family member changes numerous lives. Although there is never any real acceptance of these life-changing crimes, the loved ones can, on some level, understand that evil exists in our country. However, there is no understanding or acceptance of evil, when that evil should have never been in our country. It becomes impossible to fathom that this situation was ever allowed to happen, when a loved one discovers that this animal was allowed into this country through open borders. Or even worse, that this criminal was arrested for other crimes in America, not deported, and released back into our country because of politics.

I spoke with an ICE Officer on a San Diego Fugitive Operation Unit, and he told me that last year this unit—in the first large city north of Mexico—arrested only 170 criminals. San Diego County has a population of over 3.3 million residents, and they only arrested 170 criminal aliens! California is a sanctuary state, so the importance of ICE Officers locating and arresting illegal alien criminals is even more heightened. Because no local police departments, sheriffs, or other

California state agencies will turn over criminal aliens to ICE, these criminals are just released into our communities to further terrorize our neighborhoods.

This is a perfect example of the criminal neglect and malfeasance our own government imposes on its citizens. The primary responsibility of a government is to provide law and order to protect its citizens. Our federal government ignores their responsibilities all in the name of power and wealth.

I wish I kept a record of the number of times I arrested a previously deported criminal alien to show how many times one individual was arrested by police and sheriffs in sanctuary California between Border Patrol arrests—in other words: from the time this criminal was arrested by the Border Patrol or ICE and deported from our country to this person's subsequent successful illegal return to America and the number of times this individual was arrested by the police and sheriffs for committing other crimes before being arrested by Border Patrol and ICE again. These local municipalities often actually release these illegal alien criminals well before they serve their complete sentence, to open jail space for other degenerates in our society.

I remember numerous times while processing a criminally deported felon and looking at this complete savage standing before me, I raged internally with contempt and hatred. Not at this savage, but at the liberal lunatics that forbade their local law enforcement officers from contacting federal immigration agents when this savage was in the local law enforcement's custody. The sanctuary state of California allowed this savage, and millions like him, to rape and pillage our citizens and communities when all they had to do was call either the Border Patrol or ICE and we would have picked up this pile of human waste, placed him into federal custody, and deported him again. This is why ICE's presence is even more important than ever: the sanctuary lunacy protects the criminal who does not have the same moral code as an average human.

The absurdity of sanctuary cities and states are beyond true understanding. In 2017, California Governor Jerry Brown signed Senate Bill 54 into law. This insane law prohibited law enforcement officers from asking about a resident's citizenship. The law also prohibited California law enforcement officers from notifying federal immigration law enforcement if they had an illegal alien in custody. It did not matter if this illegal alien was a serial murderer or just a drunk driver. The height of Bill 54's absurdity was when Nancy Pelosi's husband, Paul Pelosi, was viciously attacked in his home by an illegal alien from Canada. The local San Francisco Police Department would not share any information or turn the subject over to ICE. The damage done by releasing criminal illegal aliens back into society instead of turning them over to federal immigration is unimaginable.

I just had a lengthy conversation with a San Diego ICE Supervisor about what the backend of this Immigration Parole looks like. He was so matter-of-fact when he told me that only 10 percent or less of the paroled illegal aliens self-report. He continued by saying that the 90 percent that do not self-report abscond into the fifty states and are free because there is no one that is tracking these individuals. That 90 percent equates to millions of illegal aliens.

ICE Officers tell me that the 10 percent of the paroled illegals that self-report do so in vain. The immigration system is so overwhelmed and corrupted that the ICE Officers cannot even put them on a calendar to see the Immigration Judge. The officers place these 10 percenters on a "non-detained calendar," which means these individuals will never see an Immigration Judge. I asked my source what ICE gives them. He stated that they give these paroled illegal aliens nothing. I immediately asked, what about work authorization documents? He said that is the responsibility of the United States Citizenship and Immigration Service (USCIS). He added that maybe USCIS will give them a work authorization document, but they are also overwhelmed. USCIS has over nineteen thousand employees around the world. At least 10 to 20 percent of these nineteen thousand are support personnel that have no authority or power to do anything except support the officers. Let's be generous and suppose that ten thousand USCIS Officers work in America and are the best of the best at what they do. How many of the millions of fraudulent NTAs, Asylum, Parole, and now CBP One App individuals will they be able to process this year for work authorization? Now, remember there are another three to four million people that are going to be in the same line in another twelve months. My source said the best-case scenario is if these 10 percent of illegal aliens get an attorney or help from an NGO. In almost every situation, these illegal aliens will remain illegal aliens to be used as a pawn for the elites, or they will become a criminal who will never have to fear being deported.

An article from Simon Hankinson of the Heritage Foundation[54] focuses on the absurdity of following the law as a legal immigrant, when all you have to do is cross the border and give yourself up. If you do that, you bypass all the immigration fees and the long interview and medical processes. Mr. Hankinson is a legal immigrant that followed all the protocols and procedures, but he feels like a patsy. He rightfully asks how other legal immigrants like himself feel after witnessing the unconstitutionality of ushering in people illegally—are they "Patsies? Suckers? Mugs, marks, or saps, maybe?" [55] Mr. Hankinson's perspective is unique because not only did he go through the legal immigration process, but he was a Consular Officer and knows the process as an expert. Mr. Hankinson perfectly captures my concern and resentment toward Biden and his administration's illegal efforts to parole in millions of undeserving people: "Not only is the DHS allowing millions using a parole power intended for only a few individuals, but the staff who should be working on legal petitions and credible asylum cases are being diverted to process illegal aliens at the border." Mr. Hankinson hits the nail on the head: the Biden policies hurt the people who are honoring our nation's sovereignty and waiting patiently for their turn to become legal residents and future citizens of America.

My ICE Supervisors from around the country all tell me that morale does not exist. These ICE Officers are not disgruntled federal employees just collecting a paycheck. Instead, they are extremely professional and patriotic. They fight every day to do their job. In fact, if these officers could take all the energy and thought on how to circumvent the corruption within their agency and apply it to locating and arresting illegal aliens instead, they would have unprecedented success.

All we have to do to see what that environment of support, expectations, and leadership would mean to ICE Officers is look at their productivity during the Trump years. In fact, we can go straight to the internet and see a 2017 press release that during the first one hundred days of Trump's executive order regarding immigration enforcement priorities, ICE arrested over forty-one thousand illegals. That was a 37.6 percent increase from the same time frame in 2016 when Trump had just been elected and sworn in. The ICE Acting Director, Thomas Homan, who is a true patriot and fighter, stated, "these statistics reflect President Trump's commitment to enforce our immigration laws fairly and across the board." Homan continued to describe the most important aspect of Trump's leadership: "ICE agents and officers have been given a clear direction to focus on threats to public safety and national security, which has resulted in a substantial increase in the arrest of convicted criminal aliens."[56] Trump provided leadership and guidance, and ICE was empowered. The numbers continued to increase throughout Trump's presidency, until Biden and his team tore everything to the ground.

We now go from Tom Homan, a staunch fighter for a secure and sovereign nation, to Biden's appointment of Kerry Doyle as the head of the Office of the Principal Legal Advisor (OPLA). Doyle is now supposed to be the biggest supporter of immigration and customs laws, using all her authority and power to ensure all removal cases against every sort of criminal alien is enforced. [57] Let's take a quick look at the new OPLA's work history. Doyle was the managing partner at Graves & Doyle which specialized in immigration law in the city of Boston. I am assuming she and her firm were not representing ICE Officers or Border Patrol Agents. It gets better: Doyle was the chapter chair for the New England Chapter of the American Immigration Lawyers Association (AILA). Again, there were no green uniforms in the waiting room of this law office. And it gets even better: Doyle is a strong advocate for sanctuary cities. When you look at what is happening across the southern border and along our nation's coastlines you begin to see that Ms. Doyle is in fact the perfect appointment for this position. It is devastating as an Officer and Agent working in federal immigration law enforcement knowing the enemy is not only inside your house, but strategically positioned to kill you at a moment's notice. Throughout my career, I felt like a pawn in a dirty, corrupt board game. I would have long conversations with my dad about the enemy within and how I never feared the savages that I arrested in the dark of night along the filthy border, but I feared these quislings that would Monday-morning quarterback me and destroy me, all for a chance to promote or to position themselves for future advancement.

CHAPTER 11
NGOs: Smugglers

NGOs ARE ILLEGAL alien smugglers paid by the US government. In this chapter, I will name several of these NGOs and how their partnership with the US government has been a huge success for them. I will discuss their collective mission and the enormous sums of money they receive to lobby for open borders, relocating illegal aliens north into the interior, and finally helping these illegal aliens to settle into their new homes. This assistance is not free—the American citizen foots this bill to the tune of billions. This partnership between these two entities is one of the greatest frauds perpetuated on our great nation all in the name of religion and moral self-righteousness.

I am a Catholic. I love my faith, and I believe that Jesus Christ is the son of God. I believe in the Catholic doctrines, and my faith plays an important role in my life. That said, I place no trust in the facilitators of my faith, who have been at odds with my career as a Border Patrol Agent and what I believe is the most important issue facing our republic: illegal immigration. The number one NGO in partnership with the United States government for "refugee resettlement" is the

Catholic Church. "Refugee resettlement" encompasses every aspect of illegal immigration from lobbying our government for open borders, relocating these illegal aliens across the US and the cost of resettling these individuals in our communities. Refugee resettlement is inclusive of every illegal alien no matter what their immigration situation. The Catholic Church in the United States, driven by the United States Conference of Catholic Bishops (USCCB), does all of this for a price, which, paid by the US government from 2008 to 2023, is over $3 billion and counting. Breaking that insane number down, under Trump, the Catholic Church received $212 million annually for immigration-related services, but under Biden's first year, that number skyrocketed to over $600 million. I have to wonder: Did homeless veterans, many suffering from addiction and mental illness, get $3 billion during this same period? If not, then why? And if they did, wouldn't another $3 billion that was given to the NGOs have further helped our homeless vets?

I will dive deeper into the Catholic Church and the subgroup, Catholic Charities, that the church uses to carry out these immigration services. There are tens if not hundreds of smaller NGOs that are making millions off the American taxpayer. Lutheran Family Services, Jewish Family Services, and United Way, along with the Catholic Church/Catholic Charities, are some of the biggest NGOs profiting from the Biden open border. To be honest, these players have been profiting for years off the suffering of illegal aliens and the devastation these individuals bring to our country. These NGOs launder the billions of dollars annually wasted on illegal immigration from the US government.

Spooner Mesa's Cross. Doing God's work!

The government gives grants in the tune of hundreds of millions of dollars annually to these NGOs and title these grants as "refugee resettlement." However, these NGOs use these millions of dollars for everything under the sun for the benefit of illegal aliens. My favorite investigative reporter, Michelle Malkin, wrote a book titled *Open Borders, Inc.: Who's Funding America's Destruction*,[58] where she goes into detail about the corruption of these NGOs and their partnership with the US government to undercut and destroy the demographic makeup of America. Michelle Malkin has been screaming into the wind for over a decade against the traitors that have used illegal immigration as a tool to acquire wealth and power. Her many books about illegal immigration are must reads as she has a unique and direct way of articulating the corruption, treason, and the people and organizations that monetarily benefit at the expense of America.

As you continue to read, ask yourself why every organization that inserts themselves into this mess and the very same people in governmental positions of power always seem to profit in terms of wealth, power, or both? The follow up question must be: Has America ever benefitted from this invasion?

I remember my last few months as the Deputy Patrol Agent in Charge during the first few months of the Biden administration. I instinctively knew that this was only the beginning. Every day, I would walk into the holding facility at the Murrieta Station, and it would be packed to maximum capacity. The belief that the Border Patrol just arrests Mexicans is false. Back in the day, that was the case with a few Hondurans, Guatemalans, and, of course, several MS13 El Salvadorians were thrown in the mix. In my last few months, the number of Mexicans had dwindled as individuals from around the globe that illegally entered the US had spiked. It is now routine for Murrieta Border Patrol Station to receive a bus of illegal aliens mostly from other countries. Illegal aliens are bused from state to state and from station to station, because every holding facility is at capacity. This is one way DHS creates space in the processing pipeline.

Unfortunately for America, Border Patrol Agents are extremely effective even in the face of immense adversity. With every bad policy we were given, Agents figured a way to be efficient and successful. Looking back on my career, I believe without doubt that the politicians, elites, and the weak leaders in the Border Patrol counted on this strength within the Border Patrol. As the Agents worked diligently to figure out how to manage this disaster, NGOs came in to clean up the end of this smuggling game.

The NGOs became extremely efficient as well because the more efficient they were, the more profit they make. Remember the substantial number of illegal aliens that had COVID and just walked out of their prepaid hotel and per diem? What does that do for the bottom line of the NGOs if they have to pay for fewer hotel rooms and meals? Michelle Malkin's book *Open Borders, Inc.*[59] goes into detail about the corruption of these NGOs and their partnership with the US government to undercut and destroy the demographic makeup of America. The federal government not only pays the NGOs millions of dollars annually, but also gives the illegal aliens who are claiming refugee status asylum, Immigration Parole, or are simply released, goodies such as preloaded cash on credit cards and "loans" for thousands of dollars to settle into whatever state they choose. The federal government has no mechanism to collect the repayment of these loans, so they turn these same religious and nonprofit NGOs into collection agencies, and they are allowed to keep half of everything they collect. The NGOs are not content with the billions of dollars they have been given from the federal government; they are so greedy that they shake down the illegal aliens for the loan repayment. As a Catholic, I must ask a very important question: How does Jesus feel about his faith leaders collecting payment from the very people that need the faith leader's help the most?

The impact these NGOs have on communities, as they pour thousands of illegal aliens into hotels, is profound. Felipe Rodriguez, a worker at the Row Hotel in New York City, is a whistleblower about what is happening in fourteen New York City hotels that are housing illegal aliens.[60] Exasperated with the illegal aliens living in his hotel and the way they were trashing the hotel, he stated, "It's a disgrace." He complained about issues involving domestic violence, fights between guests and hotel staff, people having sex in the stairs, consuming drugs, drinking all day, and security issues. Rodriguez also stated that the hotels have problems with many people sick with COVID, chicken pox, and other illnesses. Rodriguez stated that his hotel is a disaster; the hotel has lost all control of their property. The biggest issue I saw in this interview that struck a chord with me is that the illegal aliens feel so emboldened, because they are the ones actually in power and running the hotel. No one is holding these illegal aliens accountable.

The Row Hotel in New York City is the example of what America will look like in a short time. America will be overrun by millions of individuals that feel empowered and emboldened to demand and then take all we have to offer. These people will be conditioned by our government, these NGOs and religious organizations, and weak Americans, as they begin to expect nice hotels, food on demand, medical care, clothes, and all other amenities that the land of milk and honey has to offer. The money for all this charity will end one day. These people will have become accustomed to this way of life. When it is taken away and they are forced to provide for themselves and their families through working jobs at the lowest level of the economic ladder, these millions of people, accustomed to three prepared meals a day, housing in nice hotels with laundry service, money for drugs and alcohol, and everything else our government gives them will now have nothing. They will look up from those miserable jobs and their meager homes at the people who lied to them. They will not distinguish between the lying politicians and the average American citizen, and they will lash out in violence. We will all be affected by their collective rage that they are working for substandard wages with minimum government services because the government will be maxed out. They will feel abandoned and lied to because they were lied to and abandoned.

The majority of these illegal aliens have little to no formal education and are illiterate in English and, many times, even in their own language.[61] They will be involuntarily forced into the positions in society with no power, privilege, or hope for the future, as right behind them are millions more of their brethren who will work for less and will work longer hours. A vicious cycle of hope and excitement for a life of fantasy will end in desperation and hopelessness.

It is happening right now in New York City as Mayor Adams is trying to move all the single male illegal aliens from their nice hotel to a Brooklyn migrant relief camp: "[we are] moving single adult men from the Watson Hotel to Brooklyn Cruise Terminal, as we transition to the hotel to meet the large number of asylum-seeking families with children."[62] Single adult males are not having this. They have become accustomed to this way of life and want no part of the lower standard of living that they are being forced to accept. They are revolting and refusing to leave their hotel. This both infuriates me and makes me laugh, because men like Mayor Adams caused this situation. They are morally wrong to think giving other people's hard-earned stuff to people, who have no right to that hard-earned stuff, is compassionate and kind.

We also see this playing out in European nations like France, England, Germany, and Italy that have been invaded by illegal aliens. They were welcomed by liberals with great emotion and fanfare, as these immigrants were pawns in the Left's massive virtue signaling. As in all emotion-based decisions, reality awaits. The fanfare from Europe's Left lunatics faded away, as did much of the government assistance, and these immigrants were left standing in the street with no job, no home, and no hope except to fall into the underground economy where they will slave away for the exact same people who welcomed and showered them with love a few weeks earlier. They are tricked then betrayed by the politicians and elites of Europe.

As in America's invasion, the overwhelming majority of these European "immigrants" are single adult men. When these men are hungry, tired, dirty, and hopeless, they become violent. Many European cities are burning and pillaged by these angry men. Violent crime has spiked to unthinkable levels in Germany, Sweden, France, and more as their illegal alien population has exploded in recent years. The illegal immigrants in their country do not share European culture, way of life, religion, language, or any understanding of the function and responsibility of living in a first world country.[63]

Every day, another dozen articles pop up on my favorite news websites about another illegal alien committing heinous crimes against humanity. I could write endless books just from detailing the thousands of articles annually from newspapers, websites, and journals across this nation reporting on illegal alien crime.

Here is an article that caught my attention.[64] An illegal alien in Alabama tried to murder six individuals by burning down their house. As Robertsdale Police Lt. Paul Overstreet stated, the illegal alien "used an accelerant, gasoline, to light several mattresses on fire inside his room and causing the entire house to be filled with smoke." It gets better: the illegal alien used a bungee cord to tie the front door shut. The police responded to the burning house to find the illegal alien standing outside the home holding a gas can! Thank you, Biden and the NGOs!

Every poll that focuses on American citizen's favorability toward their own government and religious organization shows that most Americans have lost faith in our most cherished institutions. There are numerous reasons why Americans are angry, disillusioned, and resentful toward our government and religious institutions. On some level, we all feel lied to. We all feel as if we were manipulated to the betterment of the individuals that run our government and our places of worship. God built in all of us, some more than others, but we all have it: the ability to hear the truth. Truth has such a ring to it that it is unmistakable when you hear it. Conversely, we instinctively know when we are being lied to. Many times, our human nature pushes those instinctual feelings aside because we so badly want to believe that our leaders are honest and trustworthy. However, even when we push those feelings aside, we know the time will come when we will be forced to recognize the lies told to us. I believe America is waking up, but there are still large numbers of Americans that are pushing the truth aside because they want to believe everything is going to be okay. However, everything will not be okay. Ask the villagers from small towns that litter Europe's countryside if everything is okay. Ask the America ranchers and farmers on the border if everything is okay. Ask the homeless man in one of America's big cities if he is okay sleeping on the cold hard street because the shelters are maxed out. Ask the legal immigrant if she is okay having her wages depressed from illegal aliens driving wages down as she tries, in vain, to obtain the American Dream. Everyone suffers from the intentional destruction of our immigration system, except for the politicians, elites, and religious organizations disguised as NGOs as they all become more wealthy and more powerful at the demise of American citizens and the abuse of illegal aliens.

CHAPTER 12
Drugs, Disease, and Death

IN THE END of Trump's final year in office, he solemnly stated that our citizens were dying in record number from drug overdoses. That year, the United States of America, the greatest nation on earth, had over fifty thousand overdose deaths. To give context, that is almost exactly the total number of deaths in the Vietnam War. We have an incredible monument in our nation's capital honoring those soldiers. That number of fifty thousand is truly unbelievable until you realize that by the end of Biden's second year in office, that number doubled to over one hundred thousand. As we entered into Biden's third year, all data points to record numbers of overdose deaths, careening to one hundred fifty thousand. There is a direct line from the open borders facilitating easy and safe passage of hard narcotics to the record number of overdose deaths.

The drug cartels own the border and every narrow trail leading north from the border. No one crosses the border without paying for that privilege. Human smugglers are subservient to the narco smugglers and drug cartels. Human smugglers are brutal, violent, and without compassion for their loads, for these immigrants are nothing to the human smuggler but a product. The narco smugglers and cartels share the same characteristics magnified by a million. The drug cartels and the men within those organizations are savages. In this world, only the most violent person can survive. The amount of money is mind-boggling. One of the most prominent problems for the cartels is where to store their money because they can't launder the money fast enough. In Biden's administration, the money is coming in at the fastest rate ever. Large and small shipments of narcotics are coming through the open borders in record numbers.

Incredibly, these same narcotics have become even more deadly because of a synthetic opioid called fentanyl, which is mixed and cut into hard narcotics like cocaine, methamphetamine, and heroin because it is cheap. Fentanyl is created in China, shipped to the Mexican cartels, and then delivered across the open borders into the United States. Of the estimated 110,000 overdose deaths in 2022, 67 percent involved fentanyl mixed into the hard narcotics. Fentanyl is amazingly fifty times stronger than heroin and one hundred times stronger than morphine. This is what is causing the zombie-like movements of drug addicts in the large metropolitan cities across America. Philadelphia is the perfect example of what happens to America's cities from the free movement of drugs from open borders. Sara Carter, an excellent investigative reporter, did a report for Fox News showing the drug zombies roaming in open-air drug markets in Philly.[65] Ms. Carter stated the problem perfectly, "Just so you can get a perspective here, 95 percent of the narcotics here in Philadelphia, according to law enforcement sources I've spoken to today, are coming from the Sinaloa

Cartel." Drugs mixed with fentanyl straight from Mexico are landing in American cities two thousand miles from the border.

From the DEA website: "Fentanyl is the single deadliest drug threat our nation has ever encountered. Fentanyl is everywhere from large metropolitan areas to rural areas; no community is safe from this poison. We must take every opportunity to spread the word to prevent fentanyl-related overdose deaths and poisonings from claiming scores of American lives every day."[66] Young kids thinking they are taking a low-level prescription drug at a party are now dying because that prescription drug is actually a fentanyl pill.

A reasonable question to ask is why the narcotic cartels are wasting their time with people wanting to cross into America. There are two reasons.

First, alien smuggling is a multi-billion-dollar-a-year enterprise. Secondly, illegal alien smuggling distracts whatever Border Patrol and local law enforcement presence there is, so the cartels can move their loads with complete ease and assured success.

The narco cartels are no different than any other business in terms of goods, distribution, and costs. The less they are caught and the more goods they can move through uninterrupted distribution, the more money they make. It is really that simple for them. Biden has made their jobs easy. Think like a narco smuggler for a second. Imagine you work for the Sinaloa Cartel and your job is to coordinate the movement of your cartel's cocaine and heroin laced with fentanyl across the border and into the United States. Wouldn't you locate the easiest route by researching the border gaps to coordinate your shipment's crossing in unpatrolled areas of the border? Texas, New Mexico, Arizona, and some rural parts of California are wide open. As the coordinator of shipments of fentanyl-laced cocaine and heroin, you have become highly successful because there are open gaps for miles in every border state.

Just this past July 2022, the Los Angeles DEA arrested a narco smuggler moving one million fentanyl pills with a street value of almost $20 million.[67] This isn't the only bust of fentanyl for the LA DEA. In 2021, the LA offices seized over three million fentanyl pills. That is almost three times the amount from the previous year. That year would have been under Donald Trump. The year with triple the deadly pills is under Biden. This isn't just happening in California, but in all border states. In September of 2022, the Albuquerque FBI Violent Gang Task Force seized another one million fentanyl pills.[68] All the same outcomes of death and destruction that would have occurred in Albuquerque would have happened in LA if these pills were not stopped. However, and I take no joy in stating this, whatever is seized is a small fraction of what is getting away.

Unfortunately, my last statement can be proven by doing a simple Google search for "million fentanyl pills seized." This Google search could fill another three-hundred-page book! Endless articles and press briefings of border states arresting and seizing this deadly drug, but you will also see interior states showing large fentanyl seizures and arrests. States like Colorado, Kansas, Ohio, New York, and every other state in the Union. The DEA in 2022 seized over 379 million fentanyl doses. Do you see a connection to the open borders? Two decades ago, the number of people who died from synthetic opioids was fewer than one thousand.[69] This is an issue that touches every level of society. No longer are overdose deaths confined to lower-class drug addicts. Now, the reach is in all levels of the social structure. I strongly believe the number of overdose deaths will continue to rise in record-setting numbers as the border remains open. Fentanyl deaths are so out of control that the Seattle medical examiner is running out of space to store the overdoses.[70]

Reports show that the cartel business in narcotics is booming. The amount of money earned by these cartels is staggering. The cartels are now warring with their government in Mexico. Years before, the cartels would have minor but deadly skirmishes with the Mexican military. Not now. With the profits rising to higher and higher levels daily, the cartels now have the money to purchase surface to air missiles, RPGs, and any other military grade weapons. To prove my point, just look at the recent battle between El Chapo Guzman's son Ovidio Guzman Lopez and the Mexican military. It was a bloodbath with twenty-nine left dead.[71] The Mexican military had to bring in gunships to fire from the sky to battle the convoy of Sinaloa Cartel vehicles. This is not occurring in a faraway nation like Iraq or Afghanistan. No, this is happening literally across that unfinished border wall. The war to the south of us has already crossed into our nation, and it will make its way deep into America, because why not? Who or what is going to stop them?

I finally heard someone state that we must wage war on the cartels like we fought ISIS. That was President Trump in January 2023. He was correct when he stated, "Joe Biden has sided against the United States and with the cartels. Biden's open border policies are a deadly betrayal of our nation." Then, the greatest Border President in my twenty-four-year career stated, "When I am president, it will be the policy of the United States to take down the cartels, just as we took down ISIS and the ISIS caliphate."[72] The days of sitting back and hoping and praying the corrupt Mexican military, law enforcement and politicians would take care of the problem are over.

I wholeheartedly agree that we have insane people running our government, but they are more corrupt than insane. They are just as intentional about allowing narcotics to pour over into America as they are about illegal aliens. Trump stated that he would have a naval blockade to stop the maritime smuggling and that he would use Special Forces to achieve maximum damage to the cartels.[73] And why wouldn't a United States president do everything in his power to protect America and her citizens? It is stunning that this has to be discussed, then criticized, when Americans of all ages and economic positions are dying from overdoses and damaged by drug-addicted lives.

If you search "Drug Addicts in American Cities" for videos, you will see city after city with zombies walking around or standing for hours in bizarre ways, looking like scenes out of *The Walking Dead*. We send spacecrafts to Mars to take pictures and send them back to Earth, but we can't stop savages from smuggling deadly drugs into our country.

Let's talk about a taboo subject that makes the politicians and elites squirm: the numerous infectious diseases brought into our nation by illegal aliens. I have witnessed mumps, chicken pox, scabies, lice, influenza, and drug-resistant tuberculosis. There have been cases of leprosy and polio—two diseases that had been eradicated from our society for decades. We have people from all across the planet making their way into America with diseases that we didn't even know existed. Having a communicable disease is grounds for inadmissibility in Section 212 of the Immigration and Nationality Act (INA), yet every politician acts as if they have never heard of this law. Andrew Arthur's article on CIS.org makes a strong point by quoting Peter Edelstein, MD, who stated in *Psychology Today* in 2017,

> In the end, it is hard to completely ignore the health risks posed by those whose entry into the country avoids medical examination and treatment. Whether you sit on the "build the wall" end of the spectrum or the "they're just seeking a better life" end, accepting that the treatable major health risks are freely entering into our general population is an unwise strategy, regardless of your political leaning...[74]

Let me give you a personal story to drive home this point.

In November and December of 2019, we were dealing with the caravans and the final strong push of illegal aliens trying to get into America before Trump's wall was to be completed. Our cells were full as we tried to process and then deport them as quickly as we could. Our short-term holding facilities became long-term holding facilities. We averaged one hundred fifty to two hundred illegal aliens daily from numerous countries, many of whom got sick as they "stayed" with us for weeks: stomach aches, colds, pregnancies, scabies, and many other medical issues. Like every other Border Patrol station, the Murietta Border Patrol Station had contracts with local medical centers, and we had to take detainees to the local medical center's emergency room. This became an everyday occurrence, multiple times a shift. This back and forth hurt our enforcement posture, but it was part of our duties. Then the medical center's manager told the Murietta Border Patrol Agents that they would no longer take our detainees in the ER. Instead, the medical staff would meet our Agents in the back of the medical facility. We were also instructed that the detainees would be examined inside the vehicle. When we asked why, we were told that the medical staff could not effectively determine what diseases our detainees had, but whatever illness they had was not good and they could not allow our detainees to sit with their other patients in the waiting room.

In December and January, our Agents began getting sick, but we thought it was from the flu and cold season. We also knew that some of our guys got the "crud" from our detainees, which was just part of the job. I got really sick in the beginning of January. I would get crazy sick once a year from working in harsh weather and from physically handling people that had been living out in the elements for weeks, but that sickness would only last twenty-four hours. Not this time. It was so bad that I laid in bed for several days. I didn't eat, watch TV, or even move in my bed. My headache never relented, and I would go from freezing cold to fits of sweating profusely. I remember telling my wife that I had never felt this bad in my life. I had a severe cough and pain in my lungs for months.

I had what the endless flow of sick illegal aliens had in my station's holding facility—we just did not have name for it yet. We do now: COVID. The wave of COVID started in the West and made its way to the East Coast. The illegal aliens my Agents arrested, and the thousands that were bused to our station to be processed, all had COVID. A deadly disease was allowed into our country and into my station, and I brought that same deadly disease into my home where my beautiful wife and son lived.

COVID became the norm in our holding facilities. Then the Biden administration took over. That's when things got crazy, because we were forced to release these deadly, COVID carriers right onto the streets or to the NGOs, no questions asked. The Border Patrol, forced by DHS, gave these

COVID-positive individuals to the NGOs because the federal government was covering its ass. DHS knew that these NGOs would eventually release them onto the streets, but the difference was the DHS could claim ignorance or that they had done their due diligence. Either way, DHS was complicit in the deadly spread of COVID.

The DHS has a unique way of hiding the truth when it comes to illegal aliens' diseases and medical outbreaks while in our custody. The last year of my career, San Diego Border Patrol Stations were having to close down some station's holding facilities and transfer their detainees to other stations because of numerous medical outbreaks of lice, scabies, tuberculosis, and COVID. Did we turn these people back to their home countries? No, we treated their illnesses and diseases to the tune of millions of dollars or let the small-town medical centers foot the bill, crippling their finances.

In 2019, when "cages" were considered bad because Trump was the president, CNN quoted Dr. William Schaffner: "They create facilities that encourage the spread of infectious agents."[75] This doctor works for the same government that built these cages for the US Centers for Disease Control and Prevention. I wonder what Dr. Schaffner knew in 2019? Every Border Patrol Agent hates detaining these illegal aliens longer than the prescribed time, because they should either be deported or put into federal holding facilities. In this same article, CNN perfectly captured the thought process of DHS when a CBP official was questioned about what they report to health officials, "Obviously every case of scabies doesn't need to be reported or raised." Why not? Many Border Patrol stations are right in the middle of small towns and large cities. The Murietta Border

Patrol Station is a stone's throw from a large, Christian daycare. The Imperial Beach Border Patrol Station sits on the edge of a neighborhood, and Chula Vista Border Patrol Station is right in the middle of a large, residential neighborhood.

Death along the border is as normal as the sun rising. A place of extreme violence and depravity, the border is a place without compassion or a place for the weak. However, the weak always seem to be moving through this place, and they pay a heavy price. The border eats them either by her terrain or the unforgiving men who use the border as their way of making a living. A strange and unique feeling on the border, shared by the Agents and the bad guys, is a disdain for weakness. The bad guys see weakness in other men as an affront to nature, and the Agents see the weak as yet another thing that they have to protect.

Border deaths from 1998 to 2018 ranged from the mid-200s to the mid-400s. During Trump's final two years in office there were 300 deaths in 2019 and 247 in 2020.[76] Under Biden these numbers have exploded: in his first year in office, over 560 individuals died trying to cross the border. However, as he has welcomed the world to come into America, the deaths skyrocketed to 853 in 2022. CBS News captured the angst of a woman who lost her Peruvian nephew, "My nephew's death has left us devasted. It's a very tragic death, to travel so far and die in an unknown place."[77] Another statistic from CBS that gives a clearer picture of the dangers of crossing the border is the number of illegal aliens in distress that the Border Patrol rescues. In 2022, there was a 72 percent increase of rescues—22,014 lifesaving operations. The US government knows full well that more and more horrifying deaths will occur—drowning, heat exposure, murder, and suffocation—in smuggling vehicles like the fifty-three that died inside a tractor-trailer in the Texas-June heat. Drowning seems to be the death of choice, as Eagle Pass, Texas, is the new hot spot for illegal crossings. NPR quotes Manuel Mello, the fire chief: "It's basically a drowning a day that you're seeing."[78] There is a legal and orderly way to cross that does not involve rape, murder, or dying. They paid a price out of proportion to their crime, but they did make that decision, albeit at the urging of our government.

As difficult as these numbers are to fathom, they are only the deaths on our side of the border. The numbers in Central America and Mexico are unknown, but as lawless as America's border is, it's Disneyland compared to the trauma gauntlet of Central America and Mexico where murder, rape, and complete depravity rule. The dead bodies cover the border with young, five-year-olds who drowned in the Rio Grande to young men whose bodies have decayed in the brutal summer sun.

Things on the border have spiraled so out of control that local border morgues in Texas are running out of space. There are so many unidentified bodies that local morgues are resorting to trailers to store the bodies. A Maverick County funeral director stated that "he had to stack bodies as he runs out of space."[79] The deaths on the northern border are exploding as numerous illegal aliens are freezing to death as they try and traverse across the border in the winter months. This year, a family of four from India froze to death trying to cross from Manitoba to Minnesota. The children were eleven and three years old.[80] In what world does this become a normal situation where everyone involved just accepts it? The border is a place of drugs, death, and disease, making this stretch of land lawless and chaotic just as it was designed to be.

CHAPTER 13
Environmental Disaster

IN THE 1980s, the Environmental Protection Agency (EPA) declared several sites in the United States as EPA Superfunds. If we applied the same standards as in the '80s to the current situation on the border, the entire border would be labeled a Superfund site. The litter, piles of human feces, running rivers of sewage, and landscapes covered in discarded clothes, water bottles, diapers, and shoes has destroyed the beautiful border landscape. Tons of garbage litter the land as hordes of humanity run through the open border with complete disregard for America's beauty. The irony of this whole debacle is that as their countries fall into chaos, poverty, pollution, crime, and oppression. These people run from their responsibilities as citizens of their homelands, only to bring it all here. They ignore our laws and create crime. They try to escape poverty only to land in poverty here, because of their lack of education and ability to function in a first-world nation. They fear oppression but are fine with being oppressed by elites from another country. They leave third-world nations that are plagued by pollution and trash, only to come to America and desecrate our deserts, oceans, and ranches with no regard to property rights.

As I prepared to write this chapter, I decided to use articles from the last decade to the present-day to show how the ecological devastation of the border evolved into the disaster it is today. Many parts of the border are wide open deserts as well as urban areas with residential housing pushing right up to both sides of the border. There are numerous cattle ranches and farms that use the border fence or wall as their southern boundary. For the sake of argument and a solid round number, let's use ten million as the number of illegal crossers during Biden's first two years. Using wildly conservative numbers, let's assign each illegal alien one water bottle, one soda can, one bag of chips, one candy bar, and one backpack with a pair of shoes, a shirt, pants, underwear, and socks. These illegal aliens carry way more than what I just itemized; this is a low estimate of what ten million illegal aliens have brought with them into America. After they swim across the Rio Grande, walk hundreds of miles through the desert, swim around the rusted border fence in the Pacific Ocean, or run as fast as they can into wooden areas or neighborhoods, they will all discard their ten items on the border landscape. That is one hundred million items in two years, littering and poisoning the earth! A cleanup crew in Rio Rico, Arizona, pulled out over forty-two tons of trash between 2008 and 2012, in only 160 acres of the Cocopah tribal lands of western Arizona. One of the cleanup crew members, Raquel Martinez, stated, "We need more bags...there's so much trash."[81]

Think about the ecological disaster of ten million people defecating on the border. Thousands and thousands of used toilet paper rolls, millions of plastic water bottles, and millions of items of clothing—so numerous a person cannot see the dirt in the washes, trails, or hallowed-out brush. I have walked through these areas in Imperial Beach Station in California and in Douglas and Nogales Stations in Arizona. There are miles and miles of trails throughout the border that look exactly like a city landfill. A CBS affiliate in Florida did a report on a veteran named John Rouke who traveled to Eagle Pass, Texas, to coordinate a cleanup at one of the epicenters of the invasion.[82] He enthusiastically exclaimed, "Let's get this place cleaned up, man. Gotta start somewhere." Then, as with every "visitor" that comes to the border, reality smacked him right in the face. Seeing the complete situation, Mr. Rouke stated, "This is just beyond comprehension, man," and continued in amazement, "It's out of control. It has to end. I don't even want to walk any more. It just makes me sick."

I am not laughing at this man, because what he wanted to do is important. It's just that I have learned that no one really understands that alternative world that is the border.

Where is the Sierra Club? Where are the climate alarmists? I worked as a Journeyman and Supervisory Border Patrol Agent in the Imperial Beach Border Patrol Station, which is in the middle of an environmental disaster. The Tijuana River is pumped with so much raw sewage and industrial pollution, the river actually runs west to northwest, meaning its waters move upstream.

Tijuana River spilling tons of raw sewage into America.

Think about a time in your life when you witnessed a place that was so disgusting, so foul-smelling, and so repulsive that your senses were overwhelmed. That is what it is like to work in the Tijuana River Valley. All the street runoff from open sewers and business runoff in Mexico finds its way down into the Tijuana River. I always laughed at how, after a heavy rain, the Tijuana River would swell and, at times, rage with violent water currents. But days later—in the awesome sunshine of Southern California—the water levels of the Tijuana River remained the same, because the sewage spill-offs from the residential neighborhoods and businesses in Mexico continued. I used to stand guard on the border overlooking the raging Tijuana River in complete amazement as automobile frames, washers and dryers, refrigerators, dead dogs, parts of buildings, and even kitchen sinks found their way down the Tijuana River and into the Pacific Ocean. Several times a year, the Fish and Wildlife Service would respond to the Border Patrol finding a dead body on the banks of the Tijuana River.

Sewage runoff from the city of Tijuana.

In my twenty-four-year career, the beach from the border to the south end of the Imperial Beach Pier has never been open to swimmers, because of the continuous sewage spills from Mexico into the Pacific Ocean. I can pull up articles all the way back to my first days as an Agent in 1997. Just look at the description of the sewage spill of February 2017: "Between Feb. 6–23, more than 143 million gallons of raw sewage was discharged into the Tijuana River upstream in Tijuana-inevitably finding its way to the Pacific Ocean."[83]

Again, where is the Sierra Club? Where are the politicians?

Can you imagine any country deliberately dumping millions of gallons of raw sewage into another country, and then the abused country remaining silent? Why wouldn't anyone say or do something about it? Well, because our politicians, elites, and environmentalist are scared to death to point a finger at our third-world neighbor. The globalist elites and our politicians want us all to act as if everything is okay and there is nothing to worry about. By pointing a finger at their gross negligence, we would have to demand and expect changes from them. If we all stood up and pointed out the injustice of their population pouring into America, we would demand changes and adherence to our laws.

There are endless news stories about devastation to our federally protected wildlife refuges. In 2005, Mitch Ellis—who works for the US Fish and Wildlife Service as the manager of the Buena Aires National Wildlife Refuge in southern Arizona—wrote, "The Impacts of Illegal Immigration on Public Lands" about his testimony to the House Subcommittee on Interior, Environment, and Related Agencies.[84] This Wildlife Refuge covers 118,000 acres, yet in 2005, an estimated 235,000 illegal aliens crossed in this area alone. Mr. Ellis goes into detail about the devastation to the wildlife and landscape and the number of deaths, murders, and rapes that occurred in these 118,000 acres. Over 500 tons of trash were left behind by the illegal aliens, *annually*, which includes human feces and used toilet paper. The number of trails the illegal aliens cut through the refuge denuded 300 acres of vegetation. Later in the article, Mr. Ellis briefly touches on the touchy subject of human feces and used toilet paper and the profound impact that has on the environment. Again, this was in 2005. Does 2023 look better or worse? The 235,000 illegal crossing through Buena Aires in 2005 looks like child's play compared to the insanity of today.

In a world where our government ignores the people they represent and uses our taxpayer monies to fund international projects for citizens from other nations, there is no better example than the International Boundary and Water Commission United States–Mexico (IBWC).[85] The US and Mexico agreed to a joint sanitation project built in San Diego (which means the border). Here's the kicker: to treat Mexico's waste. How much is this sanitation project going to cost America for Mexico's problem? Only $330 million! The politicians yell back, "Don't worry—we made Mexico pay $144 million!" In this boondoggle of a project, Bruno Pigott, the Environmental Protection Agency Deputy Assistant Administrator for the Office of Water, and another administrator attended the signing with their Mexican EPA counterpart. What was stated by the Mexican Commissioner Adrianna Resendez was, "These efforts are expected to address a need that has prevailed for many years in the communities of San Diego-Tijuana, to solve the problem of transboundary wastewater…." What was not spoken out loud was the condemnation from our EPA officials of the intentional transboundary wastewater from *Mexico*!

International failure. Human waste pours into the Pacific Ocean.

Why is it so hard to simply state the obvious truth about our neighbors and the reality of the border? America should stand up as Trump did, yell right at the people who are the problem, and demand that they correct their behavior or America's full weight will fall hard on them. Instead, we spend over $330 million on problems of other countries. This same sanitation issue was addressed in the earlier 2000s when we spent $186 million on another sewage treatment plant to clean Mexican waste. This project failed repeatedly because the level of contaminates from Mexico was so high that this treatment center could not clean the waste properly. Our government should just burn the money instead of building treatment sites for Mexico. It would make more sense.

Imagine your neighbor has let his house deteriorate. The lawn is overgrown, and the paint on the house is peeling off. The Homeowners Association points out the problem but makes you pay for the repairs. As horrible as that is, your neighbor also browbeats you to work faster and demands that the repairs be more valuable and more beautiful than your house. In what world would that be tolerated?

The Arizona Department of Environmental Quality estimated that in 2018, over two thousand tons of trash were discarded in its state every year.[86] Today, two thousand tons is multiplied tenfold with the millions of illegals using the border trails north, to freedom and government handouts. When apprehensions decreased, so did the amount of trash, and as apprehensions increased, so did the amount of garbage left behind. Tons of diapers, water bottles, human waste, and on and on are left for the US to clean.

Let's take a suburban house and say every Friday night there is a rock concert one mile away, and every Friday after the concert the audience walks down your street, makes it a point to walk across your lawn, and use it as an outdoor bathroom, throwing and smashing their empty beer bottles against your house. In their drunken haze, they rip off their shirts and discard them on your destroyed lawn. How many Saturdays of cleaning filth off your property would it take for you to lose it and demand police presence every Friday night? Why is your safety and protection of your home more important than those of the border homeowners?

Border ranchers are past the boiling point. They feel left on their own. Laura Allen of Texas stated, "we've been doing it on our own, basically, down here in Texas. And especially down here in these border counties. We need the government to step in and get to work on this issue."[87] Another rancher in Texas who owns 1,500 acres laments the high-speed chases and the destruction to her fences and gates, and she sums it up perfectly, "It's crazy!"[88]

The other issue facing these ranchers is their safety; they are on their own for their own survival. Take the Schusters who live in the remote Kinney County and hear Mr. Schuster's angst, "The way this whole thing is shaking down and geared up from this administration is we're the victims. It's bullshit." Our government and our politicians are failing us. American sovereignty is lost, and unless a steadfast group of Americans stand up and take our sovereignty back, it will be lost for generations. These open borders and the devastation of our land is being allowed to happen solely for the elites desired demographic shift from citizens to non-citizens. It is easier to control non-citizens who are illiterate and uneducated and depend on the government for their survival.

The border has become a monument to our failures. A failure to secure our citizens' safety. A failure to protect our great nation's sovereignty. A failure to the ranchers and farmers who feed our nation, are ignored, and made unwilling victims. A failure to our assurance that our republic endures for future American generations. The probability of a government or a group of people to continually make such horrible decisions over and over again is improbable. The only rational explanation for these failures is that the decisions made regarding the border are done maliciously and intentionally. When you come to that realization and you accept that the people of this government are corrupt, you, as a citizen, have a moral obligation to stop it.

CHAPTER 14
Standing Army of Criminal Aliens

THE THOUSANDS OF terrorists blending in with the millions illegally entering our country every year is disturbing and frightening. As bad as another terrorist attack would be—and it will happen again because of the thousands of terrorists here awaiting their orders—nothing compares to the utter devastation the millions of illegal alien criminals cause annually in the United States. There is a standing army of millions of criminal illegal aliens in America.

I remember working at the Imperial Beach Station my first ten years in the Patrol and being assigned the Whiskey 2 position, a mandatory static position right on the west side of the largest port of entry in North America, the San Ysidro Port of Entry. One of the responsibilities of Whiskey 2 was calling out the number of buses that would repatriate Mexicans through a side gate back into Mexico. This was important because all the jails and prisons in the western states would turn over their illegal alien population to INS, now ICE, for deportation. The old INS, now ICE, takes those criminal illegal aliens and brings them to their final deportation location: San Ysidro Port of

Entry. I remember either being at Whiskey 2 or hearing the call over the radio throughout my ten years, "Whiskey 2 has three buses dropping off." That meant 150 criminal aliens were being deported right into our backyard and they weren't going back to their little hometowns in Mexico. No, they were going to enjoy a little freedom, get laid and drunk, then climb that border fence and try to get back into America.

Deportation buses would make the drive down "Memo Lane" to deport felons.

The calculation that I use to compute the number of illegal alien criminals living in our nation is extremely conservative, because I never want to be accused of overstating a problem; I don't have to. Even using the most conservative numbers, the number of criminal illegal aliens living in the US is unbelievable. When it comes to data on illegal aliens committing crimes, the data is purposely loose because the federal government does not want the truth of this data to ever see the light of day. Secondly, several studies have shown that local and state jails and prisons use the first claimed citizenship of the arrestee. An individual that is illegally in the country will always lie about their place of birth for fear of being deported. The longer the individual is in custody, the better chance the authorities will discover the arrestee's true citizenship. Many, if not most, of these illegal aliens are released shortly after arrest for an array of unbelievable reasons, and their citizenship is not found. The jurisdictions that these criminals are arrested in do not change their citizenship in the database after releasing the criminal and discovering their true citizenship. There were many times after I arrested a criminal alien and ran them through the national criminal database that the individual's FBI record showed them as a United States citizen.

I believe the number of illegal aliens that are being held in local, state, and federal custody is 20 to 30 percent. In some states like California, I believe there are times where that number climbs to 50 percent. There are roughly two million "beds," or jail space, throughout the nation's jails and prisons.[89] Now, we need to understand that these two million beds are not permanent ending places—they are turned over daily. There are thousands of individuals being both taken into the prison population and released from prison daily. Data shows that since 1990 to 2019 (2020 and 2021 are anomalies due to COVID), the number of individuals who were arrested fluctuates between ten to fifteen million people annually.[90] I use the lowest number of ten million arrested to prove my statement that there is a standing army of criminal aliens within our nation's borders. I will also drop my experienced and professional estimated guess of 20 to 30 percent of the prison population are illegal aliens all the way down to 2.5 percent. What does that look like? Not good!

Taking that 10 million number of individuals being arrested annually and stating that 2.5 percent of this ten million equals 250,000 illegal aliens in our prison system every year. Now, let's take the data from the Department of Justice showing ten million people arrested annually from 1990 to 2023—thirty-three years—then multiply the thirty-three years by the number of illegal aliens in law enforcement custody annually which equals 8.25 million criminal illegal aliens in our law enforcement custody since 1990.

Again, I want to play devil's advocate to ensure that I show the most conservative number of criminal illegal aliens in America. I believe there are at least 10 million criminal illegal aliens living in our country right now. However, for this exercise I will start at the thirty-three-year total of criminal aliens in our country at 8.25 million. Let's begin deducting from that incredible number 20 percent for recidivism—repeat offenders over that thirty-three-year period. Let's also take 20 percent off for individuals being deported and another 20 percent of these criminals who vanished or just died. I just watered down the insanely conservative number of 8.25 million criminal aliens over a thirty-three-year period by 60 percent, and I am left with 3.3 million criminal aliens living in our country right now.

On a side note, a criminal commits numerous crimes before being arrested. Each of these 10 to 15 million individuals arrested annually by our law enforcement officers committed, on average, another ten or twenty crimes before being arrested. If we assume the average criminal illegal alien commits ten crimes before he is arrested, that equals 2.5 million crimes committed by 250,000 illegal aliens against our American families each and every year. This does not take into account the other crimes committed by the millions of other criminal illegal aliens living in our nation.

Back to the number of criminal aliens in the US, I will even go lower to prove my point. Let's say that I am way off by a third of that 3.3 million number—2.178 million criminal aliens living in our country. That is a standing army! These criminal aliens, ranging from the most violent murderers and sexual predators who rape and abuse young children to petty criminals, are destroying our nation.

When presidential candidate Donald Trump rode the escalator down to the lobby of Trump Tower and stated that he would stop the murderers and rapists from coming into the United States of America, I believed him. However, I also knew millions of these hardened criminals were already here.

That number of 2.178 million criminal aliens is incredible when you compare it to the number of men and women in the United States military—1.35 million.[91] That number of criminal illegal aliens is even scarier when you realize the number of active law enforcement officers in the United States is 660,000 and dropping.[92]

Now, take into consideration that all these numbers will spike with tens of millions of illegals that have and will continue to cross into our country under this corrupt administration.

The Left always claims that non-citizens/undocumented individuals commit fewer crimes on average than citizens. First, even if this was true (and it is not), ask the woman after she is brutally raped if it matters that illegal aliens commit fewer crimes than citizens. Everything is good until a crime is committed against you. The Democrats are letting in criminals by the thousands every day, and the Republicans do nothing while the elites, corporate America, and fraudulent religious and nonprofits cheer for more and more individuals to pour into America. They do not care about the crime and destruction caused by these people. Instead, the enormous wealth that they accumulate and the endless levels of power they obtain are the reasons this betrayal of America continues.

Just today, I had a discussion with a stranger about the border and the violence, and I was asked, "Weren't you afraid?" I answered, "I was once when I was a new Agent. I remember that time, and that experience set the tone for the rest of my career."

Of course, this stranger followed her previous question with, "Tell me about that time."

I do not like to talk with a stranger about specific personal moments on the border because I don't know what they can handle, but I obliged. I told her about when I was just off of my trainee status and working in the 90s—a heavily wooded area about one quarter mile east of the Pacific Ocean, right on the border that butted up against a large hill called "Bunkers." There were hundreds of smuggling trails that crisscrossed the 90s and this part of the Imperial Beach Station's AOR was always busy. I was so excited to be assigned the 90s in a backup role, meaning I had no static position to man, so I was free to go anywhere the illegal alien traffic was moving. Being new also meant I had to make the most of this assignment and not allow any getaways to happen, so I could get this assignment again. I walked into the 90s as a new Journeyman Agent fresh off my Field Training Unit, ready to make my bones.

The 90s seemed to always have a low-level misty fog settle over this area. The trees, thick underbrush, and sandy trails, coupled with this fog, made the 90s eerily quiet. There was no urban noise of cars, restaurants, or people on either side of the border. The only noise came from the faint sound of crashing waves along the shoreline. We had ground sensors strategically placed throughout the 90s that would pick up seismic activity from the footsteps of illegal aliens as they traversed the border trails, and when the sun went down, we always had an infrared scope truck sitting on high points along the border. I had parked my Border Patrol vehicle out on Monument Road about a half mile away from the border.

About 11:15 that night, I heard the Imperial Beach Dispatch call out a sensor in the 90s for multiple hits through my earpiece, and immediately, the West Scope Operator with the Infrared camera began searching for the hot, green, human signatures on his monitor. The West Scope called out, "I have nine bodies walking north from that sensor. I will lose sight of this group in a few seconds." My heart jumped, and I responded, "This is India 449 [my Star Number at the time]—I'm in the area." I had a great Field Training Officer who made me walk every trail in Imperial Beach's AOR, so I knew right where I needed to be. I knew that this group would hit a literal fork in the road and they could go either way, so I ran as fast as I could to that fork in the road. I ran several hundred yards and stopped near some heavy brush at this fork in the road. I was in great shape from the academy, but my heart was pumping so hard that I could swear this group could hear it because of the dead silence in the air. I was able to catch my breath and still myself for the chaos that was about to occur.

My early field training taught me many things, but the biggest one was that every illegal alien that crossed into the Imperial Beach AOR was almost always an aggravated felon. I remember standing at this fork in the road and not really grasping the irony of me being at a "life moment" fork in the road.

As I prepared myself for this encounter with nine individuals, a voice entered my thoughts saying, "This is crazy! What am I doing?" A fear raced through my body, and I hated it. I am a big guy with a strong mind and body, and I am not a coward. This thought, reasonable as it was, caught me off guard, and I remember wrestling with it as I heard footsteps and whispers in Spanish approaching my fork in the road. I will never forget making a declaration to myself at that moment, a declaration that I would never be afraid again and that I was built for this. My heart was racing again as the footsteps got closer. The fog was hovering right above my head and a wave crashed far away, and that is when I saw the face of the smuggler walking slowly past my position. He took another two steps and turned to look down the dirt path toward the other side of the fork in the road where I was trying to conceal myself. He motioned for everyone to stop and looked right at the heavy brush I was trying to hide behind. We stared at each other for what seemed like a minute, but was only a second or two. I knew I had to charge him before he was able to determine—in the dark of night—that I was not a clump of bush, but a Border Patrol Agent. I had been taught to be aggressive and take down the smuggler hard and fast. Criminals are weak and cowards by nature. They are like wolves, powerful in packs but weak when separated. They also only understand power and violence, so I always moved decisively and with a strong purpose.

It was over in ten seconds. I arrested all nine. When the transport van got to my location, I loaded my arrestees into the van, and it drove away. As irrational as this may sound, I made a promise to myself that I would never allow that rational and reasoned fear to ever creep its way back into my thoughts. I was paid a lot of money to do this job and most importantly, I swore an oath to this country that I would protect her. When I got married and we had our son, I doubled the promise to myself and added that I would always finish my shift and no one would ever take me from my family. I became a damn good Border Patrol Agent.

As good of an Agent I became, I lost groups that crossed into my assigned AOR. I hated when that happened. It would drive me nuts when I drove home after shift and I went to bed. It ate at me, because I knew with complete certainty that in each and every group I lost, there was at least one dirtbag criminal that got away and that one criminal I failed to catch would commit numerous crimes in my country. I would witness insane criminality on the Mexican side of the border, then watch those same animals try to cross into our great nation. I read a Fox News article that brought me back to my border days and the animals I arrested that had no remorse for the pain and cruelty they inflicted on people.[93] In this article, Senator Joni Ernest (R-Iowa) was appalled at the lack of humanity on the south side of the border and the savagery making its way into America: "we heard of what they call 'rape trees,' where there are areas where the cartel smugglers will take the women and girls and, well, rape them under a tree and then take their undergarments and throw them up into the tree and hang them from the branches." That perfectly describes the type of people I encountered throughout my career.

Sadly, those type of people are already in the United States of America, and our citizens, have been paying a steep price with their dignity and with their lives for decades.

Do not, for a second, believe that because you live in a rural part of the country, you and your family are isolated enough that these criminals can't touch you and destroy your life. Even if I took the 2.5 million crimes that my conservative number of 250,000 illegal alien criminals commit annually and spread them equally across the fifty states, each state would have to deal with over 50,000 crimes each year. Again, this does not take into account the other crimes committed by the millions of criminal aliens in our communities.

The monetary cost of the crimes committed by illegal aliens—rising insurance premiums, lost production, and incarnation costs—are in the hundreds of billions of dollars annually. Remember, it's only a statistic until it is you.

CHAPTER 15
Manifestation of Treason

WHAT IS THE outcome of such treason that we are living through? We are beginning to see the fruits of our government's labor. The influx of millions of illegal aliens from the 195 nations on Planet Earth cannot be a net positive for America.

The millions of people coming through our open borders are not the best and the brightest. The vast majority are functionally illiterate in their own language and have no technical skills to work in our economy. Foreign nations, like Venezuela, are emptying their prisons and insane asylums, forcing their criminals to illegally enter our nation.[94] Diseases and medical issues like leprosy, polio, and drug-resistant tuberculosis, to name only a few, are now present in our communities. Crime is rampant in a number of our big cities, and crime in all categories is increasing daily. Terrorism is always a concern in the world and America is no different, especially as thousands of terrorists sit inside our country waiting for their instructions.

I believe there will be several manifestations of this treason from our politicians and elites. First, there will be a demographic shift in our nation within a generation. The cries of conspiracy and racism from the Left will not alter the truth. A nation cannot take in tens of millions of foreigners in a four-year period and expect no demographic shift of their current population. If America has thirty million new legal and illegal immigrants from 195 countries from around the world during the four-year Biden presidency, how could any rational person think that the demographics will remain the same? This is not a racist question. Instead, it is a rational question that, if rationally answered, would state, of course, the demographics will change. How does a willfully planned influx of illegal aliens from across the globe supposed to help this nation? What sane American voted to be replaced?

The director of research Steven Camarota and demographer Karen Zeigler from the Center for Immigration Studies did a thorough research paper on the population growth in America.[95] Their findings were shocking. They researched the total population growth in the United States during the years of 2016 to 2021. They used the Census Bureau's annual American Community Survey (ACS) as their primary data source. The last year of data available from ACS is 2021. They discovered that 77 percent of the total population growth in the United States of America for those five years was attributed to immigration, both legal and illegal, and their children born. That is incredible! Almost eight out of ten new residents in America are foreign nationals. No nation can withstand this percentage of their total population growth being from people outside of the native citizens. This report came out in March 2023, and not one single media outlet or politician has even spoken about it. Camarota and Zeigler made another unbelievable discovery from Census Bureau population estimates that ran through the middle of 2022: over 80 percent of accounted population growth was from net migration. The numbers for 2023 will be even higher than 80 percent. This should startle every American from their long slumber. At this rate, America is one full generation from a complete and total demographic shift.

Rarely is it discussed or even known that black Americans have been bypassed as the largest minority group in terms of population. Hispanics now claim that title. Did black Americans ever vote on this through their representatives? For that matter, what Americans voted to replace white Americans?

This would all be different if America voted on the issue of displacing black Americans in terms of demographics. Can you even imagine *any* politician raising this issue? That politician would be run out of town, but strangely, no politician has been run out of town as all American's voting power has been diminished and to a higher degree for black Americans.

Democratic politicians from Senator Schumer to President Biden to Nancy Pelosi have openly cheered the demographic shift in America as if it's a good thing. President Biden was giddy in interviews when he was vice president, that European whites would be a minority in the United States by 2017, "Folks like me who were of Caucasian of European descent… will be an absolute minority in America…that's a source of our strength."[96] A source of strength for who? There is never a follow up question as to why displacing a current group of American citizens for an illegal group of foreigners is good for America and good for those displaced citizens.

This could be an argument if the US was a third-world nation with societal decay, economic chaos, a dysfunctional culture, and our leaders wanted to import foreigners from highly successful nations to increase our ability to succeed. In fact, the situation is reversed. Our nation is the pinnacle of success, and our government is illegally importing individuals from the worst nations, that are war-torn economic disasters, on the planet and from cultures that have no ideals or morals in common with us. When you take even one step away from the insanity we are being forced to live in, the absurdity that is taking place on the border is so apparent that the average American should see the intentionality of it all.

One illegal alien crossing times millions!

The second manifestation of this treason will be the breaking of our social services. America is in the middle of a recession, and Americans are struggling to make ends meet. Yet with all of our country's financial insecurities, we invite millions of individuals into our country that are immediately dependent on government services. Upon the release from Border Patrol stations across America, illegal aliens will be given an iPhone, travel vouchers, and sometimes even a preloaded cash card. Every single illegal alien gets one of these goodies, and once they are settled, they receive the highest level pay from all social services with the help of the NGOs. Our own senior citizens worked their entire lives putting into Social Security, only to receive a small portion of that money back. Illegal aliens get the maximum allowed from SSI, food stamps, WIC, Section 8 housing, Medicare, free school, and on and on. Is this fair?

Border towns like El Paso and Yuma are past their breaking points. Yuma's hospitals cannot maintain their services, because the government's reimbursement rates are so low or non-existent that Yuma Regional Medical Center President and CEO Dr. Robert Trenschel stated that the business model is unsustainable. He continued to describe the dire situation regarding billing the medical center's patients, "we don't know where they're going to end up. We don't know where they go. We don't know if the name's correct."[97]

Can you imagine if you gave a local hospital a false name and skipped out on the bill for thousands of dollars? You would be arrested. It is so bad in Yuma that their officials have declared a "state of emergency" for health reasons and because thousands of illegal aliens are being street released right into the community of Yuma.

Yuma has a population of approximately ninety-eight thousand. Yuma Sector in the Border Patrol has 126 linear miles of border to protect, and most of time, if not all the time, there is not a single Border Patrol Agent conducting any law enforcement activities. Uvalde is experiencing the same issues. El Paso is the epicenter of the Texas invasion currently; it is directly north of Juarez, Mexico, a notoriously deadly city whose way of life has spilled over into El Paso.

Homelessness will increase, which will overwhelm the system and displace the most unfortunate Americans among us. Who would be okay with throwing Americans out into the cold for an illegal alien? This is happening all across our big cities right now. Washington, DC, New York City, Atlanta, Denver, Chicago, and Philadelphia are claiming states of emergency and crying for federal funds. If New York City cannot handle this, how can Wichita or Des Moines? There is no difference between what our government is doing to Americans and if I threw out my wife and son into the cold of the night to fend for themselves and took an illegal alien family into my home and fed, clothed, and provided shelter for them as my real family struggled.

The third manifestation will be the incredible rise in crime. Defund the Police movements and the release of hundreds of thousands of criminals early from their prison sentences, coupled with millions of desperate illegal aliens, means we are staring down the barrel of a gun.

The number of law enforcement officers from local, state, and federal agencies and departments are dwindling, because we have all had enough. We battled for you, we suffered injuries for you, and some of us gave everything we had including our lives to be told that *we* are the enemy. *We* are told that we are the real criminals. *We* are told to leave the profession because the nation does not need or want you. So, we did. We left and watched our nation struggle with violent crime as chaos reigns. To compound this problem, fewer and fewer individuals are entering law enforcement. I can't blame them, because if I were twenty-five years old again, I would never enter this career field in these current times. Crime will explode to unfathomable levels. This situation is what many would call the worst-case scenario. Buckle up...

Lastly, I see a nation that has allowed thousands of terrorists into our country. Customs and Border Protection (CBP) stated that in the month of December 2022, CBP arrested seventeen individuals on the terrorist watch list.[98]

As I mentioned in a previous chapter, these individuals arrested in the big "squatter" groups are the dumb terrorists. The smart ones absconding in the large open gaps on the border are here in America, waiting for their orders. Our law enforcement agencies like the FBI, CIA, DOJ, and DHS are political apparatuses that no longer have the confidence of the citizens of America. These agencies do not have the leadership or the ability to locate, surveil, and ultimately arrest these terrorists. We cannot even track unaccompanied minors who can barely walk or speak and are sexually and labor-trafficked, but we expect the same agencies to find and arrest thousands of terrorists that snuck in? Hell, if we never saw them enter America, how do we track them? In February 2023, an Iranian illegal immigrant was arrested in Texas.[99] This individual was found in a trunk of a car with four other men and not arrested by the Border Patrol, but by a Department of Public Safety Officer (DPS) in Del Rio, Texas. This seemed to be another normal, smuggling arrest until we were told that this Iranian was on our Terrorist Watchlist. Thank God that the Texas DPS was working the highway and stopped this terrorist, because the Border Patrol did not have one Agent working enforcement duties. The Border Patrol Agents are transporting, processing, and releasing illegal aliens into our country instead of performing their sworn oath duties. How many other cars were on that same highway as the Iranian terrorist loaded with more terrorists? Are we to believe that he was the only Iranian terrorist who crossed the border that day?

The Biden administration's disastrous withdrawal from Afghanistan left that nation in complete chaos. I am not defending our government's twenty-plus year war that did nothing to defend our nation, but we have a responsibility to our nation and we owed it to our soldiers to leave Afghanistan with dignity and respect. We left a fortified airport, billions of dollars of our equipment, and, worst of all, we left in the most unsafe way possible, resulting in the deaths of thirteen soldiers and even more hurt. The salt on the gaping wound is that America took in over eighty-six thousand Afghanistan refugees, many of whom have never been personally or formally interviewed.[100] Never! Remember, when I say background checks, I am talking about background checks in the US. So, of course, whoever the government did a background check on had no criminal history in the US because *they have never been in the United States of America!* When Mayorkas or Biden exclaim these refugees have no criminal history or malicious intent toward the US, it's a lie!

These refugees from Afghanistan have been housed on US military bases across the nation. These refugees have thanked us for our generosity by destroying the military bases to the tune of $270 million in damages. Complete destruction of rooms, mattresses, bathrooms, facility walls, and on and on.[101] Over thirty thousand of these Afghanistan refugees were relocated to Wisconsin by, of course, the religious NGOs. Make sure you watch closely because the media will do everything in its power to cover up the increased crime, societal decay from no shared cultural norms, and the decline of the overall quality of life.

Terrorists, as the 9/11 terrorists showed us, are patient. Time is on their side, not ours. People from Sudan, Yemen, Afghanistan, Iraq, Syria, and every other terrorist hotbed are here, and others are coming. The border is wide open, and America is doing nothing to change it. We will see terrorist events in our future. We will then trace these terrorists' footsteps all the way back to their homelands. We will discover what prompted them to make their journey to America. We will see the genesis of their journey being our traitorous president exclaiming that our borders are open, and those terrorists will see a weakness, not only in our president, but in our country and her citizens. And sadly, those terrorists will be correct.

CHAPTER 16
Sexual Abuse/Child Exploitation

LET ME START this chapter by telling you that after twenty-four years in the Border Patrol and witnessing the endless cycle of hopelessness, degradation, and human suffering, I am almost completely desensitized to it all. However, there is only one thing that causes me to pause: the sexual abuse of children. As horrible as raping or murdering an adult is, nothing compares to the life-altering abuse of a child. I hate these people from the depths of my soul.

Adding to the Trail of Tears, where Native Americans were force marched, and the Bataan Death March, where thousands of American and Filipino soldiers were also force marched away from their homes, ending in death and misery, we will remember the march of millions of individuals from countries around the globe who arrived in Central America and made the journey north to America through Mexico. In this march toward freedom and a land that offers law and order, untold numbers of people will die. Women and small children will be sexually assaulted. Even liberal news outlets like NPR, the *New York Times*, and *USA Today*, along with left leaning organizations like the WHO and Refugees International report the endless sad saga of immigrant women and children's lives being destroyed by sexual abuse and rape. Just search for "Migrant Sexual Abuses" and watch in horror as articles from years ago and present-day record this depravity. New data is claiming that 60 percent of all women and children making this march through Central America and Mexico are sexually assaulted.[102] Other reports range from 60 to 80 percent of all female and child migrants making this trek are being sexually abused.

In February 2023, former ICE director Tom Homan—who, again, is an American hero—spoke to several members of Congress on how Biden and DHS Secretary Mayorkas's open border policies have led to untold numbers of sexually abused children by pedophiles.[103] When Homan discussed how these minors are being released without proper tracking and follow up, he expressed concern: "My biggest fear is we're gonna find some of these children are living with pedophiles, some of these children will be in pornographic movies, some of these children are in forced labor. This administration opened the door." If you have listened to Homan speak, he is professional, extremely knowledgeable, and passionate. Homan continued his discussion with a powerful and an unthinkable story about a Nigerian family that crossed illegally into Texas. Sadly, this story, and numerous stories like it, is being played out daily along the border, "Just just two months ago, I was in South Texas. I was with the sheriff's department for four hours, and in four hours, we found two dead bodies. Later on, we talked to a doctor—I'm going to share this story because I want you to understand why I'm pissed off this administration intentionally opened the border." Homan continued speaking with more intensity as he described the drowning death of the twenty-month-old child of the Nigerian family as they tried to cross the Rio Grande River. "The post-mortem autopsy showed that twenty-month little girl was sodomized in every opening of her little body by the criminal cartels they're paying to cross this border." Now angry, Homan finished by echoing what I know is happening on the border, "This happens every day on that border. Someone's going to die tonight. Some young girl is going to get raped tonight. You ever talk to a ten-year-old who got raped multiple times? I have."[104]

Joe Biden has intentionally caused this mass migration by literally inviting the world into our country. As in all aspects of life, unintended consequences occur. However, I know deep in my gut that Joe Biden and his team had numerous meetings crafting this intentional destruction of America's sovereignty, and in these meetings, these Benedict Arnolds had to have had discussions on the "worst case scenario." They had to know from previous data where migrants making their trek to America were sexually abused in large percentages. Hell, all you have to do is do a Google search on migrant rapes. As one woman said in a Vice article in 2016 describing her rape, "What could I do? I endured it. I didn't have anywhere to run or anyone to turn to."[105] This administration knew that these percentages of raped and sexually abused women and children was going to exponentially explode in the numbers of women and children affected. There is no other rational understanding except that the Biden administration knew this was going to happen. If you remove the power of these illegal alien's votes, they mean absolutely nothing to the Democrats. To the Democrats, these illegal aliens are rubes, uneducated, and worse than the dirty masses of middle Americans. A mother being gang-raped by savages or a little four-year-old girl being passed around to cartel pedophiles are just events that must happen to gain power. Read that last sentence again and realize that this is happening right now as you read. It is happening all day, all night, every day, and every night.

A question must be asked: How are hundreds of thousands of women and children who have been devastated by rape and sexual abuse good for America? I am not stating that we turn a blind eye to this atrocity—no, we should stop it immediately, closing our borders and sending as much military, law enforcement, and medical personnel to these regions as needed, because we own a large percentage of this problem.

As I write this chapter, I just realized why after all these years, this affects me so much. I know with certainty, as I knew with complete confidence when I looked at a criminal alien's endless rap sheet, that there would be no justice, that the pain and suffering caused by these savage criminal aliens would go unpunished, that politics would trump everything, and that the lives of peasants and the lives of Americans are worthless in the quest for obtaining power and wealth. If I am honest with myself, I must admit that I have become desensitized, callous, and hopeless, because I have witnessed too much, which has forced me to see clearly what is happening.

Since Joe Biden became president, he has allowed hundreds of thousands of unaccompanied minors to enter into the United States—from toddlers to teenagers who their parents let be smuggled into America. Once these unaccompanied minors are here, the US government effectively becomes a pimp. We farm these kids out to the unaccompanied minors' "family members" with no way to verify that they are actually family. At the end of 2021, an explosion of over one hundred and seven thousand unaccompanied minors were in US custody, DHS released 100 percent of these children to sponsors, and over half were never seen or heard from again.[106] In March 2023, Mayorkas testified in a Senate hearing that the Department of Health and Human Services had "lost" over eighty-five thousand unaccompanied minors.[107] In this testimony, Mayorkas had a moment of moral clarity and spoke honestly when he stated that these "lost" children were being labor trafficked. We are now discovering young children working the midnight shift in meatpacking plants in Nebraska. I have a young son and the thought of him working at 2:00 a.m. cleaning blood and guts off the floor in a meatpacking plant infuriates me. If it is not okay for my son, why is it okay for hundreds of thousands of children to be exploited in harsh labor conditions? Our immigration system is so corrupt and broken that we cannot keep track of what children we have in our custody. Our government is so back-logged with these minors that they are just releasing them into the US without proper checks on the individuals we are releasing them to.

Let that sink in. Imagine the horror if the elementary school your young toddler goes to simply released your precious child to a random person who stated, "Yeah, that one there. Yeah, she's mine," and the teacher gave your kid away, never to seen again. You and the local community would want blood, and all hell would be released on that school and their administrators. But we do not care about these illegal alien unaccompanied minors; they are simply a means to an end. Because we are ignorant and do not want to know the ugly truth, there are millions of young children and women who are sexual slaves in the United States of America in the year 2023. These innocent children and poor women are sold into sex trades right in our communities. Everyone in power—the media, activists, and politicians—know with great detail that this abomination is occurring in horrific numbers, but they do worse than nothing. They continue to encourage and facilitate the mass illegal migration of these people, fully knowing untold numbers of women and children will suffer abuse and degradation.

As I prepared to write this book, I read numerous articles from prominent news sources. I would then cross-check my experiences, my sources, and my own data against these news sources. Let me tell you, I laugh at the propaganda these reporters and news sources put out. Here is one of the best examples: the ACLU, Human Trafficking Institute, and others cite data from the Department of Justice that there are between fourteen thousand and seventeen thousand five hundred individuals trafficked in the US annually. These organizations, that in another lifetime never believed anything the government said, now believe everything it says. This number of fourteen to seventeen thousand is absurd. Biden's DHS has lost over eighty-five thousand illegal alien minor children and counting[108]—they have no idea to whom they gave custody of these minor children. How is that even possible? When I ran my station in the Border Patrol, if we had one discrepancy in the processing of individuals, we would immediately locate the issue and correct it. But the DHS makes the same mistake over eighty-five thousand times and nothing is changed. Or maybe, just maybe, when you make mistakes of this magnitude, it is not an accident.

Biden and his administration, along with the politized law enforcement agencies and governmental departments, want us to believe that there are fourteen to seventeen thousand trafficked individuals in the US. Approximately one hundred fifty thousand minor children have been arrested along the southern border in fiscal year 2021, and now in February 2023, the total number of unaccompanied alien children has skyrocketed to over three hundred and fifty thousand.[109] There were more than six hundred and forty thousand-plus children and teenagers arrested by the Border Patrol between 2017 and July 2021, yet we are to believe the fourteen to seventeen thousand number is correct. Again, these numbers are reflective of who we arrest—they do not account for the millions of individuals we never even see crossing our open borders. Even if we just used the data of who we arrested, the number of minor children trafficked—not including adults who are trafficked—far surpasses fourteen to seventeen thousand.

Just from pure numbers, the amount of minor children being trafficked and raped in sex circuits across the US blows the lies from our government out of the water. But here is an even bigger point: let's say I am crazy and everything I am writing is wrong—are you ok with fourteen to seventeen thousand people being trafficked and abused in our country? Even the best-case scenario from this disastrous immigration debacle is sickening and unacceptable.

Many reputable news outlets and reporters are even claiming the percentage of raped and sexually assaulted women and children is closer to 80 percent. Even if we assume 60 percent, that number is staggering. I have four sisters and several nieces. If I randomly placed one of them in a group with nine other women making this migration trek, my sister or niece would, for certain, be raped or sexually abused.

International investigative reporter, Sara Carter, recently spoke on the Rose Podcast,[110] in detail, about her time in Central America, Mexico, and on the border, especially about the child abuse occurring from this migration. I respect Sara Carter because she tells the truth no matter how painful it is.

She described the sex rings in the United States and how the women and children are forced into these situations.

She also spoke about another insidious crime that is organ harvesting. The drug cartels are harvesting the organs of these unaccompanied children as well as using them as "body carriers" to mule their hard narcotics across the border. What is a "body carrier?" It is someone who has narcotics placed inside their body, usually a woman's vagina or a woman's or man's anus. But since the children's bodies are already open from harvesting their organs, why not put narcotics in the opening of the removed organ? Does America really want the parents who forced their children to make this trek knowing their children would meet monsters of death, rape, and organ harvesting on this trail to be living in our nation?

Here is another tough discussion to have: there have been numerous accounts of confirmed rapes and sexual assaults of women and children *in* our custody.[111] You read that right. While these children and women are in the custody of the Border Patrol, ICE, and other DHS control, we allowed these people to be abused. How could this happen? Well, when you jam over a thousand minors in a space that is supposed to hold only a few hundred people, then add that 60 percent of those same thousand minors jammed into this small space have been sexual destroyed…well, what the hell do you think is going to happen? This is the sickest part: the government has known about these sexual abuses for years and has done nothing but accelerate these situations. If you knew this had occurred countless times before this mass illegal migration took place, why in the world would you, the government, not take steps to curtail or stop this in the future? Instead of being proactive and taking measures to ensure the safety of the people you arrested, our

United States government has created an even worse condition for this type of behavior to not only continue, but also to grow to incredible numbers. Our morally bankrupt government is a criminal enterprise that has a controlling interest in the sexual abuse of women and minors. Our government is responsible for the untold numbers, exceeding millions, of lives that have been forever altered or destroyed.

Remember when you read this chapter that "our government"—per our Constitution and our founding documents—is us! So, in effect, it is we who are allowing this abuse to continue.

Pedophilia in Mexico and Latin American is off the charts, and we are importing this sickness into our country. Furthermore, the age of consent is in the lower teens, because women can't work in the fields and bring home wages for the family as a young boy/man can, so young girls must be farmed out to marriage. This is the complete opposite of our culture. Where are the feminists demanding that this practice not be allowed to enter into our nation? Better yet, where are these feminist organizations when this practice is taking place *inside* our borders by these savage pedophiles and the parents of these young teenagers?

Even if you are 180 degrees different from me on every political issue, we can have mutual agreement on the most basic moral level: protecting young children. Why would this atrocity of rape, child exploitation, and human cruelty be allowed to continue? President Biden has the same access to the information that I have and more, yet his administration pushes harder for millions more to come to America, fully knowing the immense harm that will fall upon these people. This is cruel. This is insane. This is immoral, and there will be a heavy price paid for our deliberate participation and silence in this human suffering.

CHAPTER 17
Finalizing the Smuggle: AMNESTY

THE END GAME is always amnesty. The game plan of the elites and politicians has never changed. Although it may be packaged differently. With amnesty, they get everything they set out for, and they make their illegal acts against America legal. The large majority of illegal aliens released into our nation on fraudulent asylum and parole cases will quickly time out of their quasi-legal status and become illegal aliens amendable to deportation. There will be millions of this type of illegal alien coupled with millions of getaways throughout Biden's term as president. I will hand it to the elites, they have won in the past and I strongly believe that they will win again with the largest amnesty in the history of the world unless we stop them.

The "leaders" of our country have historically slow-walked their game plan. First, they weaken the border through political rhetoric, lack of funding, and a purposefully soft immigration enforcement plan. Then, they wait as more and more illegal aliens enter our nation. These leaders watch as the inner workings of the immigration system begin to slowly grind to a halt.

This is when the word "amnesty" begins to be softly and gently spoken, floating out into the atmosphere like a trial balloon to gauge the acceptance or resistance to this idea. Both the Democrats and the Republicans hold their collective breath and watch the reaction from the citizens they represent. These politicians know that the conservative media and informed citizens will howl against amnesty, but these deceivers focus on the moderate Democrat and Republican voters and watch what their reactions will be. To combat the noise from the conservative media and voters, both parties begin to make statements in support of amnesty. The statements are always the same, just the politicians change: "We have a moral obligation to bring these individuals out of the shadows!"; "We need these hard-working and family-oriented people because they are what America needs!"; and my all-time favorite, "Diversity is our strength. Fully incorporating these people into our nation will make us stronger!"

As the cries against amnesty grow, the Left-leaning media amplifies the politicians and elites' cry for amnesty. This is when the curtain to this play is completely pulled back for everyone to see. The politicians and elites dive in head-first, and they go for broke. Amnesty instantly becomes a solution to the broken immigration system and a national security need, wrapped in a blanket of morality. Never discussed is how the people who claim to have the solution to the problem created the problem intentionally. Never discussed is how amnesty supposedly fixes the problem without closing the border. Here is the truth: these traitors bank their total plan on the disinterest and ignorance of the American citizen. Sadly, those two traits are abundant in our population.

Below is a discussion that I have had several times with liberals and RINOs (Republicans in Name Only) that perfectly articulates the insanity of amnesty. This conversation always starts once an individual finds out that I am a retired Border Patrol Agent. It goes like this:

> Liberal/RINO (L/R): I know that you must have seen a lot, but I feel sorry for these poor people who just want to come to America for a better life. Walls are racist and unwelcoming. We should welcome everyone because we are a nation of immigrants!
>
> Me: (I always hesitate because I do not want to go down this road but damn it…) Really? Everyone?
>
> L/R: Yes, everyone.
>
> Me: (Here we go…) There are over eight billion people on planet earth and over five billion live in poverty we cannot even imagine. For the sake of this conversation, let's say two of the five billion want to come and live in America. Do you agree with this?
>
> L/R: (They always agree with this statement) Yes, I agree.
>
> Me: Ok. I anoint you king, and you get to make the determination of how many of the two billion are allowed into our country. With your power, everyone allowed in America gets the complete support of the government to make their transition as easy as possible. So, how many?
>
> L/R: Well… (They always stumble at this part of the conversation).
>
> Me: Is it all two billion?
>
> L/R: Well of course not! We can't handle two billion people in our country! That's almost six times our population.

Me: One billion, one hundred million...?

L/R: Hmmmm...twenty million. I would allow twenty million to come into America. (They are always so happy when they come to this number, and they always do. I am amused because they actually think of themselves as generous in this discussion).

Me: Alright, twenty million it is. Now, as king, what are you going to do about the other 1.98 billion people trying to get into America?

L/R: (Stunned silence).

Me: You have to build a wall, right? You have to control who and what comes into America, correct?

L/R: (Continued silence as he/she tries to understand what just happened, then...) I guess you have to build a wall...

Me: Why was my wall and immigration plan racist and xenophobic when I wanted to keep out two billion people, but your wall is moral and justified when you want to keep out 1.98 billion people?

L/R: (This is where the conversation ends with either more silence or the use of bad words).

This conversation is the perfect example of the surface level of insanity this issue lives on. No one in politics or the Left-leaning media ever asks the simple questions beyond the surface level of emotions.

A video by Roy Beck from Numbers USA[112] uses gumballs to show how using mass migration into the United States as a mechanism to solve poverty in the world doesn't make sense. I recommend this video to everyone because it shows the irrationality of the whole system and the unicorn theories of open migration. In this video, he is on a stage with a table where he places several glass containers filled with gumballs. Each container represents several countries from a region of the world. Each gumball represents one million people, so there are thousands of gumballs in these containers representing the billions of people on the planet. Beck takes one gumball and puts it in a large, open, glass container representing America. He states correctly that America legally takes in one million legal immigrants annually (more accurately, 1.2 million). He states that simply bringing one million people into our country annually is detrimental to our nation and if our government takes in double that number—two million—all of our social services would break, which is confirmed by looking at the state of emergencies in New York City and DC where just thousands of illegal aliens being transported there caused chaos and destruction to their social services.

As Beck takes one gumball and places it in the glass container representing one year of legal migration into America, he also places eighty new gumballs in one of the containers representing the poor countries, because the World Health Organization (WHO) states that eighty million babies are born into poverty every single year. He repeats these two more times until America's glass container has several gumballs, but the gumballs representing the poor countries spill out of their containers and onto the floor. His brilliant point is that no matter what number America tries to import, it will never even make a dent in the world's poverty because of the population growth in those poverty-stricken nations.

Beck also made a powerful statement that almost never gets discussed: the individuals that are legally immigrating to the US are probably the more educated, skilled, and frustrated people in their home nation. He correctly points out that the individuals we allow to legally immigrate are the change agents needed in their home nations for these nations to emerge from their generational poverty. It is not mass immigration into the United States of America that will help the world end poverty. Instead, the remedy to these problems should come from the people in those countries.

Tijuana neighborhoods pushing right up onto the border. Credit: Dave Ellrod/EllrodImages.

The president of El Salvador, Nayib Bukele, states exactly what Beck articulated on the stage with the gumballs.[113] He asked how was he going to build his nation up and out of poverty if all his young, working-age men are in America. He stated that this was a huge problem for his country and demanded that Biden stop enticing his countrymen to make the trek through Mexico into the US.

Presidents on both sides of the aisle—this was President George W. Bush's favorite lie—claim that these immigrants want to be Americans. This lie was created to get Americans warmed up to the idea that the millions of people here illegally came here because they want to be a part of the American Dream. My colleagues and I have spoken to thousands of these people, and they say they all were coming to America for work and money. I would ask them point blank, "Do you want to stay here in America?" and they always answered, "No. I want to make money and return to Mexico, El Salvador, Brazil, or wherever." They love their countries in spite of their corruption and economic despair. They want the financial opportunities America offers, not the citizenship (unless that improves their financial efforts).

I remember when, right after 9/11, hundreds of Border Patrol Agents were detailed up north to New York, Boston, and other eastern locations to help with law enforcement and ensuring order and safety. My colleagues returned from this detail telling the same stories but from different locations, such as working the airports. They told me stories of complete airport terminals filled with illegal aliens they had detained who were trying to leave America and get back to their homeland. The biggest answer to the question "why are you leaving?" was: "there is going to be a war and this is not my country or my problem." The endless stories from my colleagues validated my theory that these immigrants never want to be Americans, they just want what America has to offer.

The slow rollout of the elite's immigration plan was thrown to the side once Biden stepped into the White House. The plan has been expedited. Waiting to see how Americans feel about amnesty is no longer a factor for this administration, politicians from both parties, and the elites. Instead, amnesty is openly discussed as the only option to fix this immigration mess. The same claims that the system is overwhelmed and that we need these uneducated and illiterate individuals to secure a diverse society are being screamed at us loudly and clearly.

What is unique is the pace of every segment of this plan. The Biden administration, with the help of numerous Republicans, has put this demographic shift through immigration into high gear. There is nothing on the horizon that shows this is slowing. Republican Senators Tillis, Graham, McConnell, Romney, Murkowski, and Collins—to name just a few—are working with the Democrats to push an amnesty, not just for the DREAMers but for all thirty million illegal aliens in our nation. A new Gang of Eight arose from Biden's meeting in Mexico with Mexican President Obrador and Canadian Prime Minister Trudeau. Senators Sinema (D-AZ) and Tillis (R-NC) are also trying to revive the DREAMer's amnesty—encompassing over two million DREAMers, and millions more through fraud. Of course, both Sinema and Tillis throw us crumbs of "monies for stronger immigration enforcement." I have heard this song and dance for almost three decades; it is laughable at best, insulting and frustrating at worst.

Amnesty is the final stage of the traitorous plan to fundamentally change America. If this is not being done intentionally to demographically change America for votes and wealth, tell me, why this is happening? Every time I ask people this question, they just look at me in silence. Their silence says it all. The demographic change is not about race, but about citizens versus non-citizens. This change is about control in all forms of government oversight. It is hard to control citizens who know their God-given rights spelled out on our founding documents. It is hard to control Americans fortified with their Second Amendment rights. It is very easy to have complete control over individuals who are uneducated, have no understanding of the rights of American citizenship, and have no idea that our form of government is a republic. It is also easy to control individuals who are solely dependent on government. Americans are self-reliant and demand a government that represents its people. The illegal aliens coming to America are from communist and socialist nations. Our way of life is completely foreign to them, and they have no respect or understanding of our belief in law and order. Our leaders have intentionally created this disaster, and they are winning this game for the soul of America and her future.

CHAPTER 18
Leadership

O NE STRONG LEADER can change an organization, a state, or a country.

Being a strong leader means having the ability to be consistent and fair in your approach to decision-making, knowing what success is, constantly moving forward to accomplishing that goal, and having courage to do the right thing in the face of adversity. We need a leader who embodies the characteristics of a strong leader if we are going to undo the deliberate destruction of the immigration system and the damage done to America.

The leader this country needs must have a strong and unbending moral compass whose true north is what is best for America. This leader must be unapologetically patriotic and unafraid to speak the truth, no matter how harsh and unpleasant the truth is. This will not be easy, as every vile label will be thrown at this leader for simply stating the obvious. There has been so much damage done that this leader will have to be willing to get into the weeds and make systemic changes that will garner irrational and violent responses. This leader will have to possess the characteristics of a major change agent.

I have been extremely fortunate to have had tremendous examples of true leadership in my personal and professional life. My dad was the epitome of a leader as a man, a federal law enforcement agent, a husband, and a father. There were so many leadership qualities I learned from my dad, but the one aspect that stood out the most was his quiet strength. Here was this huge bear of a man, possessing obvious size and power, and I never saw him beat his chest or do anything to draw attention to himself. Even as a little kid, there was no doubt who the alpha male was if my dad was in the room. Despite his dominating size, power, and intelligence, my dad was kind, understanding, and gentle. As calm as my dad was, my mom was the opposite; she was a whirlwind. My mom was in constant movement, running our home with six kids, but we all knew that Dad was the leader. Not in a macho domineering way, but instead, my dad led his family with his steady demeanor and the calming way he handled even the most pressing issues.

It was my dad's quiet strength that I have tried to imitate as I became a federal law enforcement agent, a father, and a husband. The famed, Canadian, psychologist Jordan Peterson made a profound statement about the need for individuals, especially men, to be "competent and dangerous and take the proper place in the world." Each time I hear Dr. Peterson say this, I think of my dad and wonder if I possess those traits. The first point of this statement is that each man must be competent in his thoughts and talents as each person has a proper place they must occupy in this world. Secondly, Dr. Peterson articulates that the competent man must be dangerous but have the ability to restrain himself to the point physical action has to be used. This statement by Dr. Peterson and his follow-up explanations of what being dangerous means describe my father perfectly. My dad could have easily pushed people around from simple size intimidation, but he never did. However, it was never lost on me, from a young kid to now as an adult, that my dad was a dangerous man.

As a young Border Patrol Agent, there was a Supervisory Border Patrol Agent named Joe that I looked up to, and I watched closely as he handled some very difficult and sensitive situations on the border. I knew that I wanted to be like Joe and earn the same respect shown to him by the men and women who worked with and for him. Several years later, I had the privilege of being selected to be on his ATV Unit, and this is where I began to make a name for myself, but more importantly, this was the time I was able to witness true leadership. When you are in the middle of chaos, making arrests, and physically fighting hardened criminals, every shift, false allegations, and accusations become part of your life. The savages we arrested were straight out of state and federal prisons, and they never wanted to go back to those places. After being arrested, they were headed straight back to their eight-by-ten cages. Their last and only card they had left to play was to make an allegation of physical abuse by the arresting officer. This is where Joe's leadership rose to the top and he took Dr. Peterson's characteristic of competence to the highest level. Joe was the most seasoned Supervisor I had ever worked for. He knew the law and policies inside and out and used them as a shield to defend his guys. We worked that border diligently and kept the savages from absconding into America and terrorizing our neighbors. Joe would protect us from our own weak leaders in the Patrol, from the unhinged civil rights groups, and from aggressive US Attorneys who wanted the scalp of a Border Patrol Agent.

I watched Joe stand tall in front of me and his guys time and time again shielding us in the face of extreme pressure. He never relented, and he saved us from those vultures who wanted our scalps. Arresting the filth of humanity on that God-forsaken border was dirty and violent. The physical act of placing handcuffs on an individual who is compliant is awkward and clumsy, even for a veteran law enforcement officer. When an individual refuses to comply and fights you, it is impossible to put those handcuffs on without using some level of force. Handcuffing that type of individual becomes a violent act. The men and women we arrested in those days in the Imperial Beach Station's AOR never complied because their freedom was on the other side of us, and they could see and smell that freedom. Joe's status among his peers and his subordinates became legendary. So much so, when his career was winding down, he left the Border Patrol with the proper nickname of "The Legend."

One of many foggy nights working on Joe's ATV Unit.

I took the lessons I learned under Joe and from my father and implemented them into my leadership style. When I took over my own ATV Unit and when I created and ran CBET, I ran those units like Joe and my dad would. My units always had Agents with very different personalities and quirks. However, they all shared two of the exact same qualities: type A and patriotic. I would use the traits my Agents possessed, and I channeled that energy into incredible success. There were times where there were hurt feelings and fights, but in adversity, we became tied to each other. Adversity in real time is not a great place to be, but all great teams must go through it. One night, a large narcotic maritime load was coming ashore north of Los Angeles and south of Santa Barbara. This was a night when adversity reared its ugly head. Everything that never happens happened. There was a new Homeland Security Investigator (HSI) Supervisor, that my unit had never met, working this night, and the Sheriff Department and the California Highway Patrol (CHP) partnerships in this area were brand-new. I had two of my best CBET Agents just miles from this panga landing site. Both were Hispanic males, one with a shaved head and the other with scraggly facial hair, and both were wearing ratty jeans and T-shirts. They looked like the twenty-plus mules and three boat captains who were smuggling narcotics.

In the Border Patrol, nicknames come with the territory, and you don't get to choose them. One of my two guys was named "Skinny" because he wore skinny jeans, and the other was named "Cherries," but the story for that nickname stays inside CBET. Skinny and Cherries were chomping at the bit to get to the landing zone and were driving like crazy to get there. I was trying to call the HSI Supervisor, but he didn't answer. I knew he and his guys were near the landing zone and most likely had no cell service. I was able to contact my Sheriff and CHP point of contact, but my point of contact couldn't get in contact with the lead Sheriff or CHP Officer on site. I was sitting on a beach two hours away in San Diego at two o'clock in the morning as my two Agents were heading into a potential Blue-on-Blue situation. Blue-on-Blue happens when one law enforcement officer or group of officers does not know another law enforcement officer or group of officers is responding to the same law enforcement event. When these different law enforcement officers show up unbeknownst to each other, many times friendly fire occurs and law enforcement officers die. It is a terrible situation when this happens.

Here I was desperately trying to coordinate with all my partners as my two guys are responding to a potential nightmare. I remember sitting in my car dialing both of my cell phones trying to get ahold of anyone in the landing zone, but nothing.

I could clearly see in my mind Skinny and Cherries running down a beach trail as the twenty-plus mules were carrying their narcotic bundles to the shoreline. I could envision Sheriffs, HSI, and CHP watching two guys running at them, having the same appearance as the mules, and having no knowledge that CBET Agents are on scene and a Blue-on-Blue incident occurring. I threw one of my phones on the passenger seat and dialed Cherries's phone. Cherries picked up and exclaimed, "Boss we are almost there!" I responded, "No! Turn around!" There was silence on the other end, then Cherries asked, "What?" then turning to Skinny, "He said to turnaround!" I could hear Skinny in the background almost come unglued. I tried to be like my father and remain calm, "This will be a Blue-on-Blue. I can't reach anyone on the ground. You have to stand down." The pushback was immediate and unlike these two, "No! No! Boss, we are almost there!" I responded very harshly, "I am not asking! I said stop and turnaround!" There was a long silence, and I continued, "Did you hear me? I want a verbal acknowledgment!" Cherries responded first and then Skinny defeatedly in the background, "Yes…"

The news of me standing down CBET Agents from responding to a huge narcotic load spread like wildfire. By the end of shift, I had taken numerous angry and confused phone calls from my unit. Because of the size of CBET, my unit of Border Patrol Agents, OFO Officers, and California National Guardsman deployed out of three different locations. We would meet every other month at the San Clemente Border Patrol Station to debrief each other and share important intelligence. I would buy pizza and Monster energy drinks, and we would talk about the new tactics and areas the smugglers were using. This was a great way to both share information on the maritime environment and grow friendships within the unit. Fortunately, we had one of these meetings already scheduled for the next shift. These were great times because we would all be together, telling war stories, and boasting about who got the most narcotics and did it with less men. That small room would be loud and buzzing with excitement. I entered this same room to silence. No one was eating or talking. It felt like someone had died, and everyone watched me as I walked to the back of the room where my desk was. This was adversity staring me in my face, but I knew I was correct in my decision to stand Skinny and Cherries down. Now I had to be a leader, stand in front of my men, and articulate why.

I do not like waiting to confront issues, so I turned around before I got to my desk and standing in the middle of the room I said, "Let me explain my decision last night..." Because of my reputation, I had a strong level of respect and trust among my team, but they needed, and quite honestly, deserved an explanation. I told my team that the driving force behind my decision was that I wasn't going to Skinny's or Cherries's families to explain why I made the horrible decision to let their boys go into a deadly situation when I knew it was deadly. I explained that as much as I hate criminals and the destruction they cause, my primary responsibility is to make decisions that protect each of them. I finished with, "I did the right thing. If this happens again tonight, I will make the same decision because that is my job and responsibility." There was an uneasy silence then one of my guys named Aaron, with all his tattoos and beard braided with rubber bands shouted, "Fuck it! That makes sense!" Everyone laughed, and all was good. Our unit grew stronger and closer that night because we understood and trusted each other on a higher level. I learned a powerful lesson:

being a leader is not only about making a tough and unpopular decision, but also about having the intellect and courage to explain why you made the decision.

    I finished my career as a Deputy Patrol Agent in Charge in San Diego Sector. My boss was Mark, who was the Patrol Agent in Charge. Mark is the most patriotic individual I have ever met. His patriotism would sound almost corny if you didn't understand that he has a deep and passionate belief that he has a responsibility to protect this nation. He swore an oath when he graduated from the Border Patrol Academy and got his badge and gun to serve this country, and he gave everything he had. His patriotism, once sounding unbelievable, was contagious. Mark was a great leader, and he was unapologetic about his beliefs in the greatness of America and our collective responsibility to protect her. When we began to feel defeated and resentful toward Biden and Mayorkas, Mark was a constant reminder that we had to move forward and do everything in our power to protect our communities and, ultimately, our nation. This was a great lesson for me, because sometimes when I see unconstitutional obstacles placed in front of me, I want to address the lawlessness and unfairness of those obstacles. But there is another route to take, and Mark would lead us down this other path. He believed that you should work around those obstacles, within policy and the law, to achieve national security, even when the odds seemed impossible to overcome.

    I look at Joe, Mark, and my dad, and I clearly understand that our great nation needs a leader like these men. We need a leader who will restrain his strength until he must use it and not hesitate when he must. We need a leader who will stand tall in the face of adversity and effectively articulate his position based on facts and undisputed truths. We need a leader who is unapologetically patriotic and loves America. Not only should this leader love America, but this leader must also feel an extreme allegiance to her and want to protect her with his life. America and her citizens deserve a leader like this. Americans must demand a leader like this.

CHAPTER 19
The Solutions

Throughout my career as a leader in the United States Border Patrol, I had one standing order: bring me all the problems, but come with a solution. I wanted to tackle problems head on. I also knew that the best solutions to almost every problem would come from the frontline guys—the Agents who had to live with all the top-level decisions. They were implementing the policies and laws handed down from above. The implementation of policy, law, or procedure always differs from the original intent—what looks great on paper is never perfect in the trenches. The problems we face today are being intentionally created to destroy our nation. Because of this intentionality, our solutions must be direct and forceful.

The best example of our government trying with all its power to eliminate the border is their endless pursuit to remove Title 42, which basically states that the government can block all immigration due to disease (such as the COVID pandemic). I do not believe Title 42, or any other mechanism, needs to be used to stop the flow of millions of illegal aliens into our country. We are the United States of America, and if something like an invasion is occurring, we, as a sovereign nation, have the right to use every means necessary to protect America and her citizens. That being said, President Trump had traitors in his own party trying desperately to keep the borders open, so he used Title 42 to block millions of people from coming into the US.

Instead of allowing Title 42 to continue, President Biden and his administration are repeatedly going to court to suspended or remove Title 42. Why, when millions of illegal aliens have already poured into our country with millions more making the trek, would you remove a mechanism that holds back hundreds of thousands of people who are living in tents along the border and waiting for its removal? Only a corrupt government set on destroying the country our founders created would do this.

What is happening on the border right now is a national state of emergency that will have profound impact on the wellness and future success of our nation. The United States citizen population only grew by a little over 1.5 million last year.[114] In less than two years, the Biden administration let in illegal aliens totaling over three times the one-year US population growth, not including at least ten times that in getaways. A seismic demographic shift is occurring at a breakneck pace. As I have proven in previous chapters, Biden has released millions of individuals into America after arrest and millions more absconding, equaling an estimated number of 7 to 10 million annually. If we take even the low estimate of 7 million illegal aliens annually entering our country and the citizen population only increases at 1.5 million annually, how do you think this ends?

Efforts to stop the invasion from continuing must happen immediately. Our nation needs a strong America First leader who is fearless and unapologetic of America's greatness. The solutions are common sense but will need a strong leader to enforce.

ALL ACTIONS WILL BE IMMEDIATE

1. The President of the United States of America will declare a National State of Emergency.

2. The United States military will be deployed to the southern and northern borders with the Border Patrol. Whatever the number of military personnel needed to stop the invasion, add 25 percent more. Military vehicles, equipment, technology, and weapons will be deployed right on the borders. All branches of the military will be used. Coastal patrols by the Navy and the Coast Guard will increase to the level needed to ensure no illegal incursions occur along our coastal borders. Not one single individual will be allowed to cross over the international borders. Whoever tries to illegally enter America will be quickly arrested, sentenced to prison, and returned to their country of origin without exception.

3. A border wall will be constructed from the Pacific Ocean to the Gulf of Mexico. All land one quarter mile north from the border will be purchased under Eminent Domain. The land between the border wall and the first allowed private structure will be a wasteland patrolled by the military and the United States Border Patrol.

4. Every individual in DHS custody will be immediately returned to their country of origin without exception.

5. A national edict will be announced that every illegal alien in our nation, including all illegal aliens fraudulently allowed into our country under the Biden Administration via Parole, Asylum, or through the CBP One App, will be given one week to self-deport. Any illegal alien located and arrested after the one-week grace period will be deported and will never be eligible for any immigration relief in the future. No exceptions.

6. All Immigration Judges will be detailed to the border where large makeshift tents serving as Immigration Courts will be constructed. These courts will run twenty-four hours a day to adjudicate all pending immigration cases outside of the one-week self-deportation time frame.

7. Once the military and the Border Patrol have complete control of the border and not one single individual can cross or abscond, Border Patrol Agents will be detailed to ICE. ICE Officers and Border Patrol Agents will locate and deport all remaining illegal aliens still in our country.

8. All immigration laws, policies, and procedures will be reviewed and revised. This review will ensure immigration laws are efficient, void of all loopholes, and every aspect of the immigration system is based in America's interest being first. Family-based admission ends, and all admission into our nation will be merit-based.

9. Only after the border has been completely sealed and all illegal aliens have been removed from our nation will we reopen legal immigration into America. There will be a strict entry/exist program as well as an employment/employee need-based immigration. All immigrants legally allowed into America will be strictly monitored with all overstays forever banned from reentry into America. We have sovereignty over our nation. We control the flow of people and goods that enter our nation.

10. Pressure will be applied to the Northern Triangle nations south of the US to stem the tides of humanity from getting to our borders. If their help is withheld or not to our standards, all foreign aid to those countries ends.

11. Mandatory eVerification will be a national law. In order to obtain employment, education, social services of any kind, non-life-threatening medical care, and others, eVerify must be used. Any state or city that refuses to comply will lose all federal funding.

All eleven solutions would not interfere, oppress, or curtail the life of an American. America would instantly become safer and prosperous. Politicians and the elite class would no longer benefit from chaos that hurts America. America would have control over her sovereignty and her future. The individuals who come into our country will enter safely and with protections in place for them to become a part of our great nation. Every side wins, except for the power-hungry politicians and the unscrupulous elites who will no longer be able to use us as pawns for their wealth and power accumulation.

I am an optimist by nature. However, as I have gotten older, I have become more of a realist. I want to believe this treason against our nation will be confronted and destroyed, but the reality is that the corruption within our government and the elites that circle around the power structure is so deep and so entrenched I do not have much hope. If this treason is confronted, I do not see the powerful giving away their treasure without a fight. Patriotic Americans must stand strong in the face of verbal assaults and physical violence, for the powerful will use everything at their disposal to win because we have allowed them to win for so long.

The citizens who demand the country's demographics remain the same (except for natural growth from American citizens) will be vilified and canceled and become enemies of the state. As harsh as that reality is, the reality of idly standing by and hoping and praying for the best, will no longer suffice. Patriotic, strong-willed men and women will have to take the lead. Our leaders must be bold and unapologetic in their beliefs. The nation can no longer ignore this truth and assume life as we know it will continue. Instead, silence, fear, and unwillingness to get into the fight will make you as complicit as the enemies that foster this destruction.

As I tell my eleven-year-old son, "Joseph, everything has a cost. You pay with either your time, talent, or treasure." Millions of Americans will have to make that decision for themselves as to what side they are on and to what cost they are willing to pay. Our government and its elite partners are bringing the fight to us. Americans: you will be forced to choose a side, so choose wisely. This is all coming to a head, and when it all washes out, what is left will be the country in which we will all be forced to live.

The cost of our great nation is worth all my time, all my talent, and all my treasure. America is great because of her citizens. America's future depends on her citizens.

ENDNOTES

[1] Norma E. Cantu, "Living on the Border," Smithsonian Education, accessed May 22, 2023, https://smithsonianeducation.org/migrations/bord/live.html.

[2] John Binder, "Biden's Sanctuary Country," Breitbart, January 2, 2023, https://www.breitbart.com/politics/2023/01/02/bidens-sanctuary-country-fewer-30k-illegal-aliens-deported-american-communities-2022/.

[3] John Binder, "More than 1.2m Fugitive Illegal Aliens Remain Living across U.S. Despite Having Final Deportation Orders," Breitbart, January 3,2023, https://www.breitbart.com/politics/2023/01/03/more-than-1-2m-fugitive-illegal-aliens-remain-living-across-u-s-despite-having-final-deportation-orders/.

[4] Elliot Spagat and Nomaan Merchant, "Over 4,000 migrants, many kids, crowded into Texas Facility," AP New, March 31, 2021, https://apnews.com/article/joe-biden-immigration-texas-59d0eafb23d135f901dfc50ff326cfcd.

[5] Andrew R. Arthur, "Biden's Shocking About-Face on Unaccompanied Alien Children," Center for Immigration Studies, December 30, 2022, https://cis.org/Arthur/Bidens-Shocking-AboutFace-Unaccompanied-Alien-Children.

[6] Clara Migoya, "Yuma mayor declares local emergency due to 'humanitarian and border crisis,'" AZ Central, December 9, 2021, https://www.azcentral.com/story/news/local/arizona-breaking/2021/12/09/yuma-declares-local-emergency-due-unprecedented-number-migrants/6455505001/.

[7] "Emergency Proclamation Still in Place," City of Yuma, December 21, 2022, https://www.yumaaz.gov/Home//Components/News/News/1210/308.

[8] John Binder, "Biden's DHS," Breitbart, January 3, 2023, https://www.breitbart.com/politics/2023/01/03/bidens-dhs-no-records-on-over-350k-border-crossers-released-into-u-s/.

[9] Binder, "Biden's DHS."

[10] "Yale Study Finds Twice as Many Undocumented Immigrants as Previous Estimates," Yale Insights, September 21, 2018, https://insights.som.yale.edu/insights/yale-study-finds-twice-as-many-undocumented-immigrants-as-previous-estimates.

[11] Steven A. Camarota, "New. Data: Illegal Population Up Two Million Under Biden," Center for Immigration Studies, November 7, 2022, https://cis.org/Camarota/New-Data-Illegal-Population-Two-Million-Under-Biden.

[12] Camilo Montoya-Galvez, "U.S. shelters received a record 122,000 unaccompanied migrant children in 2021," CBS News, December 23, 2021, https://www.cbsnews.com/amp/news/immigration-122000-unaccompanied-migrant-children-us-shelters-2021/.

[13] [[Link not found]] https://www.fairus.org/blog/2023/04/04/biden-administration-calls-asylum-system-broken-wont-use-their-tools-fit-it

[14] "Alejandro Mayorkas," Influence Watch, accessed May 22, 2023, https://www.influencewatch.org/person/Alejandro-mayorkas/.

[15] Robert Law, "Mayorkas Tells Lawmakers Border is Secure," Center for Immigration Studies, May 2, 2022, https://cis.org/Law/Mayorkas-Tells-Lawmakers-Border-Secure.

[16] Brittany Bernstein, "Chip Roy Accuses Mayorkas of 'Ignoring the Actual Truth' of the Border Crisis," National Review, April 28, 2022, https://nationalreview.com/news/chip-roy-accuses-mayorkas-of-ignoring-the-actual-truth-of-the-border-crisis/.

[17] Neil Munro, "Border Chief Mayorkas: Laws 'Regrettable' Limit Cheap Labor Migration," Breitbart, March 30, 2023, https://www.breitbart.com/immigration/2023/03/30/border-chief-mayorkas-we-want-more-migrants-fill-u-s-jobs/.

[18] Randy Clark, "Exclusive: Biden Admin Stops Title 42 Expulsions for Venezuelan Migrants in Two Texas Border Sectors," Breitbart, April 7, 2023, https://www.breitbart.com/border/2023/04/07/

[19] exclusive-biden-admin-stops-title-42-expulsions-for-venezuelan-migrants-in-two-texas-border-sectors/.

[19] Diana Roy, "Crossing the Darién Gap: Migrants Risk Death on the Journey to the U.S.," Council on Foreign Relations, June 22, 2022, https://www.cfr.org/article/crossing-darien-gap-migrants-risk-death-journey-us.

[20] Robert Kraychik, "Exclusive—Michael Yon: 'Our Government' Funds 'Weaponized Migration' Aimed at America, Europe," Breitbart, March 23, 2023, https://www.breitbart.com/radio/2023/03/23/michael-yon-govt-funds-weaponized-migration/.

[21] Neil Munro, "Biden's Border Chief Shuts His Deadly Trail in the Panama Jungle," Breitbart, April 12, 2023, https://www.breitbart.com/economy/2023/04/12/Mayorkas-shuts-his-deadly-migrant-trail-in-the-panama-jungle/.

[22] Munro, "Biden's Border Chief Shuts His Deadly Trail."

[23] Anna Diamond, "The 1924 Law That Slammed the Door on Immigrants and the Politicians Who Pushed it Back Open," Smithsonian Magazine, May 19, 2020, https://www.smithsonianmag.com/history/1924-law-slammed-door-immigrants-and-politicians-who-pushed-it-back-open-180974910/.

[24] History.com Editors, "President Coolidge signs Immigration Act of 1924," History, November 16, 2009, https://www.history.com/this-day-in-history/coolidge-signs-stringent-immigration-law.

[25] Megan Myers, "Americans frightened by shock poll on diminishing importance of traditional values," Fox News, April 1, 2023, https://www.foxnews.com/us/americans-frightened-shock-poll-diminishing-importance-traditional-values.

[26] Mark Krikorian, "Ted Kennedy on Immigration," National Review, May 18, 2007, https://www.nationalreview.com/corner/ted-kennedy-immigration-mark-krikorian/.

[27] https://www.thegatewaypundit.com/2023/01/joe-biden-grant-mass-amnesty-work-permits-30000-new-illegal-immigrants-month-stephen-miller-demands-house-gop-open-impeachment-inquiry/

[28] Jim Hoft, "Joe Biden to Grant Mass Amnesty and Work Permits to 30,000 New Illegal Immigrants a Month – Stephen Miller Demands House GOP Open its Impeachment Inquiry," Gateway Pundit, January 5, 2023, https://whitehouse.gov/briefing-room/speeches-remarks/2023/01/05/remarks-by-president-biden-on-border-security-and-enforcement/.

29 Mark Levin, *The Mark Levin Show*
30 Matt Vasilogambros, "Noncitizens Are Slowly Gaining Voting Rights," Stateline, July 1 2021, https://www.pewtrusts.org/en/research-and-analysis/blogs/stateline/2021/07/01/noncitizens-are-slowly-gaining-voting-rights.
31 Vasilogambros, "Noncitizens Are Slowly Gaining Voting Rights."
32 Mike LaChange, "Mayor Eric Adams Says New York City At A 'Breaking Point' As Migrants Continue To Arrive At Record Page," Gateway Pundit, January 14, 2023, https://www.thegatewaypundit.com/2023/01/mayor-eric-adams-says-new-york-city-breaking-point-migrants-continue-arrive-record-pace/.
33 Gabriel Hays, "Mayor Bowser slammed for complaining that DC can't handle migrant relocation to VP Harris' house," Fox News, September 17, 2022, https://www.foxnews.com/media/mayor-bowser-slammed-complaining-d-c-cant-handle-migrant-relocation-vp-harris-house.amp.
34 Cristina Laila, "Watch: Texas Governor Greg Abbott Hand-Delivers Joe Biden a Letter During His Drive-By Photo Op Visit to the Border—Here's What It Says," Gateway Pundit, https://www.thegatewaypundit.com/2023/01/watch-texas-governor-greg-abbott-hand-delivers-joe-biden-letter-drive-photo-op-visit-border-says/.
35 Gwenn Friss and Denise Coffey, "Migrants flown to Martha's Vineyard may move to Cape Cod military base: What we know," Cape Cod Times, September 14, 2022, https://www.capecodtimes.com/story/news/2022/09/14/gov-ron-desantis-sends-undocumented-immigrants-to-marthas-vineyard-unannounced/10383220002/.
36 Steve Holland, Ted Hesson, and Dave Graham, "U.S. would accept up to 30,000 migrants a month in expanded programs-sources," Reuters, January 5, 2023, https://www.reuters.com/world/us/biden-planning-visit-us-mexico-border-2023-01-04/#:~:text=WASHINGTON%2C%20Jan%204%20(Reuters),U.S.%20and%20Mexican%20officials%20said.
37 Julio Rosas, "A Democratic Governor Is Planning to Send Migrants to NYC and Chicago," Townhall, January 3, 2023, https://townhall.com/tipsheet/juliorosas/2023/01/03/one-democrat-state-has-had-enough-of-the-influx-of-illegal-immigrants-n2617825.
38 Jonh Binder, "Democrat Mayor Declares 'Emergency' over 0.01% of Biden's Record-Breaking Illegal Immigration Arriving in Denver," Breitbart, December 18, 2022, https://www.breitbart.com/politics/2022/12/18/democrat-mayor-declares-emergen-

cy-over-0-01-of-bidens-record-breaking-illegal-immigration-arriving-in-denver/.

39 Bradford Betz, "Democrat NYC Mayor Adams calls on federal government to play more proactive role to secure border," Fox News, January 15, 2023, https://www.foxnews.com/politics/democrat-nyc-mayor-adams-calls-federal-government-play-more-proactive-role-secure-border.

40 Julio Rosas, "A Democratic Governor Is Planning to Send Migrants to NYC and Chicago," Townhall, January 3, 2023, https://townhall.com/tipsheet/juliorosas/2023/01/03/one-democrat-state-has-had-enough-of-the-influx-of-illegal-immigrants-n2617825.

41 "Remarks by President Biden, Prime Minister Trudeau, and President López Obrador in Joint Press Conference," White House, January 10, 2023, https://www.whitehouse.gov/briefing-room/speeches-remarks/2023/01/10/remarks-by-president-biden-prime-minister-trudeau-and-president-lopez-obrador-in-joint-press-conference/.

42 "Remarks by President Biden, Prime Minister Trudeau, and President López Obrador in Joint Press Conference," White House, January 10, 2023, https://www.whitehouse.gov/briefing-room/speeches-remarks/2023/01/10/remarks-by-president-biden-prime-minister-trudeau-and-president-lopez-obrador-in-joint-press-conference/.

43 Brittany Bernstein, "Chip Roy Accuses Mayorkas of 'Ignoring the Actual Truth' of the Border Crisis," National Review, April 28, 2022, https://www.nationalreview.com/news/chip-roy-accuses-mayorkas-of-ignoring-the-actual-truth-of-the-border-crisis/.

44 Brittany Sheehan, "Chip Roy's Border Bill 'Abolishing Asylum' Draws GOP Opposition," RedState, January 21, 2023, https://redstate.com/brutalbrittany/2023/01/21/chip-roys-border-bill-abolishing-asylum-draws-gop-opposition-n692243.

45 Andrew R. Arthur, "'CBP One' App Will Have Real Blood on Its Metaphorical Hands," Center for Immigration Studies, January 26, 2023, https://cis.org/Arthur/CBP-One-App-Will-Have-Real-Blood-Its-Metaphorical-Hands.

46 Associated Press, "Biden administration quietly deploys facial recognition to process asylum seekers," KVIA, June 4, 2021, https://kvia.com/news/border/2021/06/04/biden-officials-quietly-deploy-facial-recognition-to-process-asylum-seekers/.

47 Wendell Husebø, "Joe Biden Blames Republicans for Border Invasion, Claims Partisan Hostility Is Problem," Breitbart, January 5, 2023, https://www.breitbart.com/politics/2023/01/05/joe-biden-blames-gop-border-invasion-claims-partisan-hostility-problem/.

48 Wendell Husebø, "Joe Biden Blames Republicans for Border Invasion, Claims Partisan Hostility Is Problem," Breitbart, January 5, 2023, https://www.breitbart.com/politics/2023/01/05/joe-biden-blames-gop-border-invasion-claims-partisan-hostility-problem/.

49 Ronald Reagan, "January 5, 1967: Inaugural Addredd (Public Ceremony)," Reagan Library, accessed May 22, 2023, https://www.reaganlibrary.gov/archives/speech/january-5-1967-inaugural-address-public-ceremony.

50 Ian Hanchett, "FL Sheriff: We Warned Feds Migrant Surge Was Coming, Now It's Hurting Our Safety, Breitbart, January 5, 2023, https://www.breitbart.com/clips/2023/01/05/fl-sheriff-we-warned-feds-migrant-surge-was-coming-now-its-hurting-our-safety/.

51 Chris Enlow, "National park is forced to close after being overwhelmed by migrants—and the local sheriff knows exactly who to blame," Blaze Media, January 3, 2023, https://www.theblaze.com/news/florida-national-park-closes-migrant-crisis.

52 Kurt Zindulka, "At Least 19 Suspected Terrorists Snuck into UK in Small Migrant Boats: Report," Breitbart, April 11, 2023, https://www.breitbart.com/europe/2023/04/11/at-least-19-suspected-terrorists-snuck-into-uk-in-small-migrant-boats-report/.

53 Jessica M. Vaughan, "Deportations Plummet Under Biden Enforcement Policies," Center for Immigration Studies, December 6, 2021, https://cis.org/Report/Deportations-Plummet-Under-Biden-Enforcement-Policies.

54 Simon Hankinson, "A Legal Immigrant's Lament: Biden's 'Parole' Scheme Makes 'Patsies' of Those Who Abide by Law," Heritage Foundation, January 17, 2023, https://www.heritage.org/immigration/commentary/legal-immigrants-lament-bidens-parole-scheme-makes-patsies-those-who-abide.

55 Hankinson, "A Legal Immigrant's Lament."

56 Keegan Hamilton, "Soaring ICE arrests under Trump are only the beginning," Vice, May 18, 2017, https://www.vice.com/en/article/a3j9g5/soaring-ice-arrests-under-trump-are-only-the-beginning.

57 Jon Feere, "Biden's New ICE Appointee Wants Criminal Aliens Kept in Our Communities," Center for Immigration Studies, September

58 Michelle Malkin, *Open Borders Inc. Who's Funding America's Destruction?* (Washington, D.C.: Regnery Publishing, 2019).
59 Malkin, *Open Borders Inc.*
60 [[link not found]] https://www.foxnews.com/media/migrants-drinking-all-day-having-sex-in-stairs-taxpayer-funded-new-york-hotels-whistleblower.am
61 Jason Richwine, "Immigrant Literacy," Center for Immigration Studies, June 21, 2017, https://cis.org/Immigrant-Literacy-Self-Assessment-vs-Reality.
62 Aubrie Spady, "Illegal migrants refuse to leave NYC hotel for Brooklyn migrant relief center, sleep in the street," Fox News, January 30, 2023, https://www.foxnews.com/politics/illegal-migrants-refuse-leave-nyc-hotel-brooklyn-migrant-relief-center-sleep-street.
63 John R. Lott Jr. and James Varney, "Europe Shows a Clear Link Between Immigration and Crime—Like the One the U.S. Seriously Downplays," Real Clear Investigations, December 1, 2022, https://www.realclearinvestigations.com/articles/2022/12/01/europe_shows_a_clear_link_between_immigration_and_crime_-_like_the_one_the_us_seriously_downplays_867625.html.
64 John Binder, "Illegal Alien Accused of Setting House on Fire, Trying to Burn Six People Alive," Breitbart, January 6, 2023, https://www.breitbart.com/politics/2023/01/06/illegal-alien-accused-of-setting-house-on-fire-trying-to-burn-six-people-alive/.
65 Charles Creitz, "Liberal city's open-air drug crisis spiraling out of control, fueled by Mexican carels: 'We're zombies,'" Fox News, January 20, 2023, https://www.foxnews.com/media/liberal-city-open-air-drug-crisis-spiraling-control-fueled-mexican-cartels-zombies.
66 "Fentanyl Awareness," DEA, accessed May 22, 2023, https://www.dea.gov/fentanylawareness.
67 "DEA Los Angeles Field Division Makes Historic Seizure of Approximately 1 Million Fentanyl Pills," DEA, July 14, 2022, https://www.dea.gov/press-releases/2022/07/14/dea-los-angeles-field-division-makes-historic-seizure-approximately-1.
68 Curtis Segarra, "FBI: Recent Albuquerque fentanyl bust was largest ever," KRQE, accessed May 22, 2023, https://www.krqe.com/news/crime/fbi-recent-albuquerque-fentanyl-bust-was-largest-ever/amp/.

69 Tom Howell Jr., "Body count keeps growing in America's fentanyl crisis as Washington grasps at solutions," Washington Times, January 22, 2023, https://www.washingtontimes.com/news/2023/jan/22/body-count-keeps-growing-americas-fentanyl-crisis-/.

70 Jack Philips, "Seattle Medical Examiner Running Out of Space to Store Bodies Due to Fentanyl Overdoses: Official," Epoch Times, January 24, 2023, https://www.theepochtimes.com/seattle-medical-examiner-running-out-of-space-to-store-bodies-due-to-fentanyl-overdoses-official_5004888.html.

71 "Ovidio Guzmán-López: Twenty-nine killed during arrest of El Chapo's son," BBC, January 6, 2023, https://www.bbc.com/news/world-latin-america-64179356.

72 Brooke Singman and Adam Shaw, "Trump vows to deploy US special forces, military assets to 'inflict maximum damage' on cartels," Fox News, January 5, 2023, https://www.foxnews.com/politics/trump-vows-deploy-special-forces-military-assets-inflict-maximum-damage-cartels.amp.

73 Brooke Singman and Adam Shaw, "Trump vows to deploy US special forces, military assets to 'inflict maximum damage' on cartels," Fox News, January 5, 2023, https://www.foxnews.com/politics/trump-vows-deploy-special-forces-military-assets-inflict-maximum-damage-cartels.amp.

74 Andrew R. Arthur, "Infectious Diseases Making the Border Crisis Worse," Center for Immigration Studies, March 13, 2019, https://cis.org/Arthur/Infectious-Diseases-Making-Border-Crisis-Worse?gclid=Cj0KCQiA8t2eBhDeARIsAAVEga2NaKtxEl1xt4uezjG1AOHE5KinrQoaPE_KxWew2EzDZXpvMBBHhEkaAhEiEALw_wcB.

75 Elizabeth Cohen, John Bonifeld, and Minali Nigam, "CBP refuses to publicly reveal how many migrants are sick with contagious diseases," CNN, August 23, 2019, https://amp.cnn.com/cnn/2019/08/23/health/cbp-migrants-contagious-diseases/index.html.

76 Priscilla Alvarez, "First on CNN: A record number of migrants have died crossing the US-Mexico Border, CNN, September 7, 2022, https://amp.cnn.com/cnn/2022/09/07/politics/us-mexico-border-crossing-deaths/index.html.

77 Camilo Montoya-Galvez, "At least 853 migrants died crossing the U.S.-Mexico border in past 12 months—a record high," CBS News, October 28, 2022, https://www.cbsnews.com/news/migrant-deaths-crossing-us-mexico-border-2022-record-high/.

78 Joel Roce and Marisa Peñaloze, "Migrant deaths at the U.S.-Mexico border hit a record high, in parts due to drownings," NPR, September 29, 2022 https://www.npr.org/2022/09/29/1125638107/migrant-deaths-us-mexico-border-record-drownings.

79 Taylor Delandro and Robert Sherman, "Migrant deaths overwhelming border town morgues," NewsNation, accessed May 22, 2023, https://www.newsnationnow.com/us-news/immigration/border-coverage/migrant-deaths-overwhelming-border-town-morgues/amp/.

80 John Lauritsen, "Illegal crossings increasingly at U.S.-Canada border despite dangerous, deadly conditions," CBS News, February 16, 2023, https://www.cbsnews.com/minnesota/news/illegal-crossings-increasing-at-u-s-canada-border/.

81 Tim Gaynor, Migrant trash piles up at remote U.S.-Mexico border areas," Reuters, January 29, 2012, https://www.reuters.com/article/us-immigration-usa-trash/migrant-trash-piles-up-at-remote-u-s-mexico-border-areas-idUSTRE80S0QB20120129.

82 Albert Pefley, "Veteran heading to Texas to pick up tons of trash," CBS 12 News, September 5, 2022, https://cbs12.com/news/local/john-rourke-veteran-heading-to-texas-to-pick-up-tons-of-trash-september-5-2022.

83 Surfrider Foundation, "Tijuana River: The Largest Sewage Spill We've Ever Seen," Surfrider, March 2, 2017, https://www.surfrider.org/coastal-blog/entry/tijuana-river-the-largest-sewage-spill-weve-ever-seen.

84 Mitch Ellis, "The Impacts of Illegal Immigration on Public Lands," U.S. Fish & Wildlife Service, accessed May 22, 2023, https://www.fws.gov/testimony/impacts-illegal-immigration-public-lands.

85 Julia Giarmoleo, "U.S. and Mexico agree to invest $272M to address Tijuana River sewage problem," EPA, August 18, 2022, https://www.epa.gov/newsreleases/us-and-mexico-agree-invest-474m-address-tijuana-river-sewage-problem.

86 CIS, "Trash at the Border Highlights the Environmental Cost of Illegal Immigration," Center for Immigration Studies, September 19, 2018, https://cis.org/Immigration-Studies/Trash-Border-Highlights-Environmental-Cost-Illegal-Immigration?gclid=Cj0KCQiA8t2eBhDeARIsAAVEga2eOZtdGnnkuKEZGDUhs7VYG-7Z14WkFVFLDDof_y5egJIoPVXEwBAUaAnCCEALw_wc.

87. Kayla Bailey, "Texas ranchers blast Biden's obligatory border visit: 'A little too late,'" Fox News, January 7, 2023, https://www.foxnews.com/politics/texas-ranchers-blast-bidens-obligatory-border-visit-little-late.amp.
88. Sandra Sanchez, "'Got-aways,' migrant smugglers frequently damage property far from border, Texas ranchers lament," BorderReport, accessed May 22, 2023, https://www.borderreport.com/immigration/got-aways-migrant-smugglers-frequently-damage-property-far-from-border-texas-ranchers-lament/amp/.
89. Wendy Sawyer and Peter Wagner, "Mass Incarnation: The Whole Pie 2022," Prison Policy Initiative, March 14, 2022, https://www.prisonpolicy.org/reports/pie2022.html.
90. Erin Duffin, "USA – number of arrests for all offenses 1990–2021," Statista, October 19, 2022, https://www.statista.com/statistics/191261/number-of-arrests-for-all-offenses-in-the-us-since-1990/.
91. "U.S. Military Size 1985–2023," Macrotrends, accessed May 22, 2023, https://www.macrotrends.net/countries/USA/united-states/military-army-size.
92. Erin Duffin, "Number of law enforcement officers U.S. 2004–2021," Statista, October 11, 2022, https://www.statista.com/statistics/191694/number-of-law-enforcement-officers-in-the-us/.
93. Kelly Laco, "Ernst says human smugglers 'taunting' law enforcement by 'brutally' raping young girls at border, urges action," Fox News, July 20, 2022, https://www.foxnews.com/politics/ernst-says-human-smugglers-taunting-law-enforcement-brutally-raping-young-girls-border-urges-action.amp.
94. "Rep. Nehls Asks Mayorkas to Secure Borders from Released Venezuelan Prisoners Among Caravans," Office of Congressman Tory E. Nehls, September 23, 2022, https://nehls.house.gov/media/press-releases/rep-nehls-asks-mayorkas-secure-borders-released-venezuelan-prisoners-among
95. Steven A. Camarota and Karen Zeigler, "Estimating the Impact of Immigration on U.S. Population Growth," Center for Immigration Studies, March 27, 2023, https://cis.org/Report/Estimating-Impact-Immigration-US-Population-Growth.
96. Jess Sosnoski, "Joe Biden 'Whites will be an ABSOLUTE minority in America—that's a source of our strength,'" Vimeo, accessed May 22, 2023, https://vimeo.com.

97 Ian Hanchett, Yuma Hospital CEO: Providing Care To Migrants Is 'Unsustainable' for Us, We Can't Collect Because 'We Don't Know Where They Go,'" Breitbart, December 24, 2022, https://www.breitbart.com/clips/2022/12/24/yuma-hospital-ceo-providing-care-to-migrants-is-unsustainable-for-us-we-cant-collect-because-we-dont-know-where-they-go/.

98 Bob Hoge, "28 People on the FBI's Terror Watch List Captured at Southern Border Since October," RedState, January 21, 2023, https://redstate.com/bobhoge/2023/01/21/38-people-on-the-fbis-terror-watch-list-captured-at-southern-border-since-october-n692206.

99 Spencer Broen, "Why One Illegal Immigrant Captured in Texas Should Set Off Biden's Alarm Bells," Townhall, February 1, 2023, https://townhall.com/tipsheet/spencerbrown/2023/02/01/iranian-on-terror-watch-list-entered-us-from-mexico-report-n2619000.

100 John Binder, "Biden's 50K Afghans Cost Taxpayers $189M in Damages to U.S. Military Bases," Breitbart, January 14, 2023, https://www.breitbart.com/politics/2023/01/14/bidens-50k-afghans-cost-taxpayers-189m-in-damages-to-u-s-military-bases/.

101 Brad Williams, "Fort McCoy and other military bases seek millions to fix damages attributed to Afghan refugees," WIZM News Talk, December 29, 20232, https://www.wizmnews.com/2022/12/29/fort-mccoy-and-other-military-bases-seek-millions-to-fix-damages-attributed-to-afghan-refugees/.

102 John Binder, "Biden's 50K Afghans Cost Taxpayers $189M in Damages to U.S. Military Bases," Breitbart, January 14, 2023, https://www.breitbart.com/politics/2023/01/14/bidens-50k-afghans-cost-taxpayers-189m-in-damages-to-u-s-military-bases/.

103 Breccan F. Thies, "Former ICE Director: Mayorkas 'Opened the Door' to Pedophiles, Child Pornography, Forced Labor," Breitbart, February 8, 2023, https://www.breitbart.com/politics/2023/02/08/former-ice-director-mayorkas-opened-the-door-to-pedophiles-child-pornography-forced-labor/.

104 Ibid.

105 Anna-Cat Brigida, "'I Didn't Have Anywhere to Run': Migrant Women Are Facing a Rape Epidemic," Vice, August 29, 2016, https://www.vice.com/en/article/evgg9j/i-didnt-have-anywhere-to-run-migrant-women-are-facing-a-rape-epidemic.

106 Bethany Blankley, "Biden administration lost track of thousands of unaccompanied minors who entered U.S. illegally in 2021," The Center Square, February 10, 2022, https://www.thecentersquare.com/florida/biden-administration-lost-track-of-thousands-of-unaccompanied-minors-who-entered-u-s-illegally-in/article_dfae43c6-8904-11ec-af84-03cf15976aa7.amp.html.

107 John Binder, "Biden's DHS Admits Many of the 85K Lost Migrant Children Released into U.S. Are Being Labor Trafficked," Breitbart, March 30, 2023, https://www.breitbart.com/politics/2023/03/30/bidens-dhs-admits-many-of-85k-lost-migrant-children-released-u-s-being-labor-trafficked/.

108 Binder, "Biden's DHS Admits Many of the 85K Lost Migrant Children Released into U.S. Are Being Labor Trafficked."

109 Amelia Cheatham and Diana Roy, "U.S. Detention of Child Migrants," Council on Foreign Relations, March 27, 2023, https://www.cfr.org/backgrounder/us-detention-child-migrants?gclid=Cj0KCQiAic6eBh-CoARIsANlox84KRbcWSVCwqdDAWB99_6R5s8xKmpBwuaC_ABCfC4bWvygeBvO3KkYaAkLwEALw_wcB.

110 Cristina Laila, "Sara Carter Joins Rose Unplugged to Discuss Biden's Border Crisis: Sex Trafficking, Child Organ Harvesting, Drug Smuggling and More," Gateway Pundit, December 20, 2022, https://www.thegatewaypundit.com/2022/12/sara-carter-joins-rose-unplugged-discuss-bidens-border-crisis-sex-trafficking-child-organ-harvesting-drug-smuggling-audio/.

111 Matthew Haag, "Thousands of Immigrant Children Said They Were Sexually Abused in U.S. Detention Centers, Report Says," New York Times, February 27, 2019, https://www.nytimes.com/2019/02/27/us/immigrant-children-sexual-abuse.html.

112 "Immigration, world poverty and gumballs," Sustainable Population Australia, July 21, 2018, https://population.org.au/video/immigration-world-poverty-and-gumballs/.

113 "President of El Salvador talks immigration crisis with Tucker Carlson," Youtube, March 17, 2021, https://m.youtube.com/watch?v=_pAzth4f-vs.

114 "Census Bureau Projects U.S. and World Populations on New Year's Day," United States Census Bureau, December 29, 2022, https://www.census.gov/newsroom/press-releases/2022/new-years-day-population.html.

ABOUT THE AUTHOR

J.J. CARRELL RECENTLY retired from the United States Border Patrol after a twenty-four-year career as a Deputy Patrol Agent in Charge. Carrell brings a different view on immigration and on what is now transpiring in this forgotten and unknown place known as the border.

Carrell supervised an All-Terrain Vehicle (ATV) unit on the San Diego-Tijuana border between 2008-2009, the most violent time in recent Border Patrol history. In 2009, he also created the Coastal Border Enforcement Team (CBET), the most successful landside and maritime narcotic and human smuggling unit in the Border Patrol. In the five years Carrell was the supervisor of CBET, they arrested and seized numerous Sinaloa Cartel narcotic loads, and one of his Agents testified against and helped secure a conviction against Joaquín Guzmán, a.k.a. "El Chapo."

Carrell is proud of his career and the relationships that were forged with fellow Agents during the dark and violent nights on the border and along the Pacific Coast.

Made in United States
Troutdale, OR
03/08/2024